PHOTIS LYSANDROU

DOLLAR DOMINANCE

Why It Rules the Global Economy and How to Challenge It

BRISTOL
UNIVERSITY
PRESS

First published in Great Britain in 2025 by

Bristol University Press
University of Bristol
1–9 Old Park Hill
Bristol
BS2 8BB
UK
t: +44 (0)117 374 6645
e: bup-info@bristol.ac.uk

Details of international sales and distribution partners are available at bristoluniversitypress.co.uk

British Library Cataloguing in Publication Data
A catalogue record for this book is available from the British Library

ISBN 978-1-5292-4970-5 hardcover
ISBN 978-1-5292-4971-2 ePub
ISBN 978-1-5292-4972-9 ePdf

Cover design: blu inc
Front cover image: Stocksy/Jakub and Jedrzej Krzyszkowski
Bristol University Press uses environmentally responsible print partners.
Printed in Great Britain by CPI Group (UK) Ltd, Croydon, CR0 4YY

FSC
www.fsc.org
MIX
Paper | Supporting responsible forestry
FSC® C013604

In memory of my sister Tonia
14 July 1960–18 February 2024

Contents

Acknowledgements

I wish to first thank Ellen Pearce, commissioning editor at Bristol University Press, and Izzie Green, assistant editor at Bristol University Press, for the extensive help and advice they have given me through all of the successive stages in getting this book published. I also wish to thank Gail Welsh and Kelly Winter at Newgen for their invaluable help in producing this book. I thank Giorgos Gouzoulis, Marika Lysandrou and two anonymous referees for their helpful comments on earlier drafts of this book. Finally, I would like to thank the many members of my family, and most notably my wife Yvonne, for the warm encouragement and support given to me during the course of writing this book.

Introduction

Capitalism became a fully globalized system by the start of the 21st century. No sooner had it done so than it was hit by severe crises, the first being the financial crisis of 2007–8, followed by the COVID-19-generated crisis of 2020–1, and then by the crisis triggered by Russia's invasion of the Ukraine in early 2022, the ramifications of which continue to unfold at the time of writing. There is no doubting the degree to which these crises have heightened disorder, dislocation and fracture in the global capitalist system, words that have understandably figured prominently in publications discussing its current state. What is in doubt is whether this disorder and dislocation will reach the point where the system will simply not be able to function as an operative totality in any meaningful sense. The successive crises have certainly amplified centrifugal pressures in global capitalism at both the individual level as its member governments have increasingly turned inwards and prioritized domestic interests in an effort to contain the economic and social fallouts of the crises, and at the collective level as groups of governments have increasingly made their own regional trading arrangements. But does this mean that there is no centripetal force that is preventing individual countries or groups of countries from spinning off to the extent of occupying their own separate domains? The crises have also certainly helped to promote the further de-centring of the West in the production and trading spheres, a process already set in train by the West's ongoing de-industrialization and transfer of manufacturing jobs to China, India and other parts of Asia. But does this mean that global capitalism now has no operational centre of any description? These are very broad questions but the answers to them ultimately depend on the answer to one very specific question, which is whether the crises that have severely shaken the very foundations of global capitalism will, on that account, also shake the foundations holding up the US dollar's dominance as an international currency.

For much of the second half of the 20th century, those foundations were provided by US production and trading strengths, but in experiencing the same combination of de-industrialization and manufacturing job transfer as have other Western nations over recent years, the US has seen both a steady decline in its percentage share of world production and a sharp deterioration in its trade accounts. Yet despite the United States' deteriorating macroeconomic fundamentals, the dollar's international dominance has remained consistently secure, as evidenced by the Bank for International Settlements' (BIS) triennial surveys of foreign exchange and over-the-counter derivatives transactions. When, for example, the results of the latest survey were published in November 2022, they showed that while daily foreign exchange turnover had grown to about $7.5 trillion as compared with the $6.6 trillion figure that had been registered in the 2019 survey, the US dollar's share of the new figure had remained stable at around 44 per cent, a percentage share substantially larger than that of any other major currency and one that positively dwarfed the shares of the emerging market economy currencies that, even when aggregated together, amounted to no more than 13 per cent of the total. A popular explanation for this apparent anomaly, and one inspired by the lesson of history, is to highlight the role of inertia: just as the pound sterling lost its top position in the currency hierarchy not when Britain lost its top position as an industrial power towards the end of the 19th century but when the United States decided to face outwards and assume leadership of the capitalist world at the end of the Second World War, then so also will the dollar suffer the same fate at the point when other countries are ready to take advantage of the United States' deteriorating economic fundamentals and make a concerted effort to bring about the dollar's dethronement. Russia's invasion of the Ukraine in early 2022 is widely seen as having signal importance in this context because, following the sanctions imposed on Russia that included the withdrawal of all dollar facilities to it, there was now going to be a more determined effort on its part and that of its allies in the BRICS (Brazil, Russia, India, China and South Africa) association to drop the dollar in favour of alternative currencies for foreign trade and investment purposes. On this logic, it follows that while there was no change in the dollar's percentage share of daily foreign exchange turnover as shown in the BIS's 2022 triennial survey, this having appeared so soon after Russia's invasion of the Ukraine, we are likely to see a discernible change in future triennial surveys.

The predictions of a coming end to dollar dominance have been countered by arguments that highlight the importance of the size of US domestic capital markets. Along with the globalization of capitalism following the collapse of communism in the closing years of the 20th century, another paradigmatic shift in capitalism has been its financialization following the rapid scale growth of the world's equity and bond markets. It is a measure of that rapidity that where the combined outstanding value of world equity and bond stocks in 1980 was approximately $11 trillion, a sum on a par with that for world gross domestic product (GDP) in that year, by 2000 their combined outstanding value was about two and a half times that for world GDP, a ratio replicated in 2020. Throughout all this time, the United States had been by far the principal supplier of these securities, on average accounting for about 40 per cent of total global securities stocks, a figure not matched by any other advanced market economy let alone by the world's emerging market economies that, even when taken together, have on average accounted for about 15 per cent of these stocks. As is well explained, international investment flows form the basis for the close connection between the commanding size of US equity and bond markets and the international dominance of the dollar: if the world's investors are attracted by the various advantages offered by the sheer depth, diversity and liquidity of US capital markets, they obviously need dollars to access those markets and it is this use of the dollar in an international investment capacity that then links in with the role of the dollar in a number of other international capacities, ranging from its use as a vehicle and trade invoicing currency in the private sphere to its use as an exchange rate anchor and reserve currency in the official sphere. In short, what is well explained is that the foundations of the dollar's continuing dominance now lie in the realm of finance rather than in the industrial realm as was previously the case.

What is not so well explained is whether the dollar's new finance-related foundations possess the same solidity as did its previous production-related foundations. As material goods and services have intrinsic value, there was obviously never any reason to question the solidity of the dollar's foundations when these were supplied by the United States' predominant position in world trade and production. That there is now a questioning of the dollar's foundations that today rest on the United States' position as the world's leading supplier of equity and debt securities follows just as obviously because these securities, having no intrinsic value, can only maintain a value storage capacity on condition that their issuing organizations are able to maintain the necessary financial returns and because it is the deterioration in the United States' macroeconomic accounts that puts this ability in doubt. Thus, just as foreign investors can on the one hand be attracted by the size of US securities markets, which are comparatively far larger than those hosted by other countries, they can on the other hand be repelled by the thought that the size of the United States' outstanding securities volumes may be too large when set against its shrinking share of world production and weakening trade position. This failure to convincingly demonstrate the solidity of the dollar's new foundations is critical because it leaves the door open to the idea that these foundations, by virtue of being finance-related, are highly fragile and that all is that needed to cause their collapse is to subject them to sustained external pressure. In the end, it is this belief in the fragility of the dollar's financial foundations that gives Russia and its allies confidence that the dollar can be, and soon will be, dethroned.

The fact is that the dollar's dethronement is not going to happen any time in the foreseeable future because its foundations are indeed solid and will long remain so. The reason why this fact is not widely recognized lies in the failure to recognize the remarkable transformation undergone by financial securities as a consequence of the new standards and codes of conduct now in place in the financial markets. Where the funding needs of banks, non-bank corporations and governments are the principal supply-side drivers of the continuing scale growth of world securities stocks, it is the investment needs of pension funds and other institutional asset managers that are the principal demand-side drivers of this scale growth. Asset management has become in many countries a mass industry catering for the retirement and other welfare arrangements of large sections of the population, and with this development has come a corresponding growth in the demand for investables in which clients' monies can be stored and from which monies can be extracted to pay clients. Although there are other types of investable assets that serve as stores of value for asset managers, financial securities necessarily comprise the majority proportion of their portfolios because what sets them apart from other asset classes is their ability to combine a value storage function with liquidity. Now, as securities have no intrinsic value, it follows that it is only through their prices that they can acquire a value storage capacity, and as these prices are nothing other than the discounted values of future cash returns, it follows that they can only be made tangible enough to hold a determinate quantity of value over time on condition that cash returns are regularly made at the required rates and at the required intervals. It is to ensure this regularity that institutional asset managers have, through sheer lobbying pressure, forced the introduction of new cash return rules and constraints that are far tighter than anything seen in the past. In so doing, it may have been no part of their intention to see these new rules and constraints give solid underpinning to the dollar's continuing dominance in the modern era, but this is precisely what has happened.

The logic is this. Corporations and governments issue financial securities on the promise to return cash. In the absence of tight cash return constraints, these securities always remain in danger of remaining just promissory notes, empty air, but with the imposition of these constraints they are transformed into genuine stores of value. From being particles without matter, securities become particles filled with matter and what this means is that when all the securities of a country's organizations are aggregated together, this aggregation gives that country's financial markets mass and a corresponding power of attraction: the greater the mass, the greater the power of attraction, and nowhere is this power greater than that exerted today by the US financial markets. We have noted that the United States, at one end of the spectrum, currently accounts for about 40 per cent of global equity and bond volumes, while, at the other end, all the emerging market economies put together account for about 15 per cent of these volumes. But significant as these size differences are, they are nothing as compared with the differences when these are translated into currency terms, for while the United States' outstanding securities volumes exist as a single, same currency mass of dollar securities, those of the emerging market economies shrink to vanishingly small fragments when disaggregated according to their local currencies. In a world of strict international capital controls, the different sized currency financial markets can continue to operate independently of each other. But that world has gone. In line with the steep volume growth of the world's securities stocks has come a corresponding relaxation of capital controls with the result that the vast majority of the world's small currency financial markets are now subject to the gravitational force of the dollar market with international portfolio flows being the major conduit through which that force is transmitted. Only by building up its domestic financial markets to a size large enough as to make them a centre of gravity in their own right can a country or region see its currency escape the power of the dollar. The importance of this argument cannot be over-emphasized because no other lines of escape from the dollar's power are today possible, least of all being those that rely on the forlorn hope that among the huge shocks to global capitalism dealt by global crises will be a loosening of the dollar's grip on the world's currencies.

In expanding on this point, let us first recall that the globalization of capitalism following the collapse of communism did not thereby see the emergence of a globally unified capitalism centred on one country. Rather, the entry of a diverse range of countries into the capitalist sphere, coupled with the ongoing advances in transportation and communication technologies that have substantially reduced the costs and frictions of geographical distance, saw instead the fracturing and dislocation, and indeed the 'de-centring', of global capitalism. As has been pointed out in such publications as those of Buzan (2011) and Buzan and Lawrence (2014), ours is not an era of the 'superpower', as was the United States in the capitalist West and the USSR in the communist East in the aftermath of the Second World War, but an era of several competing 'great powers'. A notable development in the geo-economic sphere, one that forms the central theme in the current literature on the 'new state capitalism' (see, for example, Alami and Dixon, 2020; Alami et al, 2022; van Appledorn and de Graaf, 2022), is how national governments have expanded their policy arsenal to give their countries and their corporations, in particular, better survival chances in what has become as much a highly competitive as a highly fractured global capitalist system. As highlighted by Ikenberry (2024), the geo-political sphere has also been characterized by increasing fracture and division as different regional country coalitions have very different political views as to how the world should be ordered and as to what type of guiding rules need to be in place. Given the already fractured state of global capitalism at the turn of the millennium, it was inevitable that the damaging effects of global crises starting with those of the financial crisis of 2007–8 would only serve to further compound that fracture. This was the central theme of Helen Thompson's book, *Disorder: Hard Times in the 21st Century*, that appeared in early 2022. One of the strengths of the book is that it singles out the degree to which the control over the production, supply and distribution of oil has been, and continues to be, a key determining factor in the global balance of economic and political power. This said, its major weakness is that it does not deal with the implications of global crises for the dollar's dominance in the international currency hierarchy. The middle section of the book certainly discusses fracture and dislocation in the economic and financial spheres of global capitalism, but the discussion here mostly deals with very general issues such as, for example, how the growth of the offshore eurodollar market in the 1960s and the break-up of the Bretton Woods system of fixed exchange rates in the early 1970s were among the longer-term structural causes of the financial crisis of 2007–8. What this section does not do, as we say, is to focus attention on the specific question of dollar dominance. This omission in a book that carries the single word 'disorder' as its major title has to be of some consequence in that it gives the strong impression that the only effects of global crises are those amplifying fracture and dislocation in global capitalism, an impression that then clears the way for the idea that it is only a matter of time before that fracture and dislocation spreads from the production and political spheres of capitalism to its currency sphere, thereby ensuring the dollar's dethronement.

Contrary to this, once it is understood that the dollar's dominance now rests on its huge backing mass of US government and corporate securities, and that these securities have solidity as stores of value, it then becomes clear that the cumulative impact of the crises afflicting global capitalism at the start of this century has been not to erode that dominance so much as to have the diametrically opposite effect of further consolidating its foundations. Consider the point that institutional investors need to hold the bulk of their portfolios in the form of financial securities, assets that can potentially combine a safe value storage capacity with liquidity. Ever constant in normal times, this need becomes even more pressing in times of economic turbulence and ensuing uncertainty, and, as the United States is best placed to supply securities that can provide investors with safe value storage facilities on the scale required, it is this country that benefits the most from any rise in international portfolio flows seeking safe harbour. Consider also the point that what helped to drive the volume growth of world securities supplies in the closing decades of the last century was the growing array of financial pressures bearing down on governments and corporations. To these pressures must be added the huge costs of coping with the economic and social consequences of the global crises breaking out at the start of this century. Now, while these crises cause major organizations everywhere to increase their rate of security issuance to help them accommodate the ensuing costs, it is those of the United States that are able to make this increase on a disproportionately greater scale in that the contemporaneous heavy inflows of portfolio funds seeking safety serve to keep down US borrowing costs even while US borrowing volumes continue to grow to new heights. Thus, by causing economic and social disruption and hence an investor flight to safety, successive crises serve to continually widen the size asymmetry separating US capital markets from those of all other regions, and it is precisely this widening size asymmetry that continually strengthens the dollar.

To declare that dollar dominance is secure is not to celebrate that dominance or to condone it. On the contrary, there are many important reasons why the current unipolar currency system should be ended given the exorbitant privilege it

ONE

Financialization and the Gravitational Force of the Dollar

History teaches that a currency's leading position in the international currency hierarchy rests on the issuing country's leading position as an industrial power: when the latter is lost, so also is the leading position of the currency in question. This was the experience of the British pound sterling. It is not, however, the experience of the US dollar. When the dollar finally pushed the pound off its top spot at the end of the Second World War, the United States had by then become the capitalist world's sole economic superpower, accounting for about one half of its production and about one third of its trade. In stark contrast, the US share of world gross domestic product (GDP) has today dropped to less than a quarter and its share of world trade to about one tenth, a ratio further negatively compounded by the increasing dominance of US imports over exports. Yet this relative deterioration in the United States' underlying macroeconomic fundamentals has not had the slightest effect on the dollar's international dominance, as evidenced both by its commanding share of foreign exchange transactions in the private sphere (44 per cent of the current daily forex turnover figure of $7.5 trillion [BIS, 2022])[1] and its commanding share of currency reserves in the official sphere (around 58 per cent of the current world total figure of $13 trillion [IMF, 2024]). If the past history of capitalism's trajectory as an international economic system offers no guide to the dollar's current dominance, it is clearly because there have been some entirely new developments that have impacted that trajectory.

Two such developments stand out. The first is the globalization of capitalism following the collapse of communism. Rather than reinforce dollar dominance, however, this development should have had the opposite effect, given that the entry of the ex-communist countries into the capitalist system has served not only to further depress the United States' share of world GDP but also to further worsen its trade balance. We must therefore to turn to the second new development, which is the 'financialization' of global capitalism. While this term tends to be used in a very broad sense to denote the growing size and weight of the financial sector relative to the real sector,[2] we shall here use it in the narrower sense of denoting the growth in the size of the world's capital markets relative to the size of the world's product markets. Certain regions in certain earlier periods of capitalism may have witnessed sudden upsurges in the size of the capital markets and in the scale of their activity, as for example in the United States in the 1920s before the stock market crash and the onset of the great depression. But what is without precedent at the start of the 21st century is the relentlessly widening gap between world bond and equity volumes on the one hand and world GDP on the other. At the end of 1980, the outstanding nominal value of world securities volumes was approximately $11 trillion, a sum on a par with nominal world GDP for that year. It is safe to say that at no prior date in history was there ever such parity at that world level. Conversely, at no point since that date has the rate of growth of world GDP kept up with that of world securities supplies. Thus, by the end of 2000 their combined outstanding nominal value was about one and a half times that for nominal world GDP ($80 trillion versus $33 trillion), a ratio replicated in 2020 ($203.2 trillion versus $87.8 trillion). Now, once one looks at the percentage breakdown of the global bond and equity volumes according to country of issuance, there should be no mystery as to what sustains dollar dominance in the contemporary era, for while the dollar's 44 per cent share of daily forex turnover volume is out of all proportion to the United States' current contribution to world GDP, it is on the contrary almost in direct proportion to this country's contribution to world securities stocks, 41 per cent of the $126.2 trillion world bond volume outstanding at the end of 2022 and 39 per cent of the $106.2 trillion world equity volume outstanding at that same time (SIFMA, 2023). Further confirmation of the importance of the current finance-related foundations of dollar dominance would appear to be given by the contrasting data regarding the emerging market economies' (EMEs) position in the global financial sphere, for while their combined 13 per cent share of daily forex turnover is out of all proportion to their rising shares of world production and world trade, it is, on the contrary, almost in direct proportion to their continuing low percentage share of world security volumes.

While the new finance-related foundations of dollar dominance are widely recognized, it is also widely assumed that these foundations cannot sustain that dominance for long. There are essentially two reasons for this assumption. One is that it is not clear that the continuing scale growth of the world's capital markets serves any valid economic purpose. If it does not, there may come a time when that scale growth is reversed, in which case the dollar's dominance must also be eventually reversed. The other reason is that contemporary opinion is split as to whether the heavy use of the dollar by foreign agents in a variety of international roles will continue to be as heavy now as it was in the past, given that the dollar's international position rests less on the United States' production and trading strengths than on the size of its domestic capital markets. As this latter reason is by far the more problematic one standing in the way of finally resolving the matter of the dollar's dominance over the longer term, we shall devote the bulk of our discussion over the following chapters to addressing it. This said, it helps if we begin by briefly addressing the question of the functionality of financialization.

The first point to note in this context is that it is not as easy to explain the financialization of capitalism as it is to explain its globalization. Whatever its many serious defects, capitalism has one major functional advantage over all other socio-economic systems based on the associative, face to face principle, namely, its ability to promote economic efficiency to a greater extent than can be done by any of these other systems. If any final proof of this point was needed, it was provided by the sudden implosion of the Eastern European command economies in 1989–90 following decades of economic stagnation. By contrast, it is difficult to see how economic efficiency can be the principal driving force behind the financialization of capitalism. At the root of this difficulty is the premise that finance fulfils only one basic function, which, in Robert Merton and Paul Brodie's classic definition, is 'to facilitate the allocation and deployment of economic resources across time and space in an uncertain environment' (Merton and Brodie, 1995: 4). All branches of the economics profession concur with this premise, but where there is a divergence of opinion is over the aggregate size that the financial sector needs to reach to be able to facilitate the allocation and deployment of economic resources. While mainstream economists generally hold the view that the larger is the financial sector the more cost-effectively it can make this facilitation, a view which helps to explain why these economists tend not to use the term 'financialization' to characterize the growing weight of finance in global capitalism, most heterodox economists hold the contrary view that the current size of the financial sector is far in excess of the minimum required to enable it to serve the real sector. What seems to confirm this contrary view is that there is nothing historically new about the various ways and mechanisms through which the financial system executes its resource-allocative support role. If in all previous periods the financial sector was perfectly capable of providing these support mechanisms without excessively increasing its size relative to the real sector, the observation that there is now such an excessive increase can be construed as an abnormality, a deviation from the usual norms of capitalism in that rather than finance serving the interests of production, production is being squeezed to serve the interests of speculators and rentiers. To quote Alessandro Vercelli: 'According to most streams of heterodox economics, the process of financialization is mainly a pathological process of evolution within capitalism that requires that capitalism be radically reformed or superseded' (Vercelli, 2013).[3]

Our position regarding the current size of the global financial markets coincides with the heterodox position on two counts: first, that a substantial part of this size is in excess of that required to facilitate the efficient allocation and deployment of resources and, second, that this excessive part of finance is somehow symptomatic of self-promoting finance, finance serving finance. Where we disagree with heterodox economists is the designation of the entirety of this excessive part of finance as dysfunctional in the sense that it has more to do with serving the interests of rentiers than those of producers. On the contrary, much of this excessive part does have functional purpose, as becomes clear when recognizing that the financial markets now fulfil a second basic function that is quite distinct from their resource-allocative support function. To understand this second function, consider the capacities for production and service provision possessed by the corporations and governments that are today the major producers and service providers in most domestic economies: then, if the traditional function of the financial markets is to help facilitate the efficiency with which these capacities for production are deployed by facilitating the efficient allocation of the resources required by these capacities, the new additional function of the financial markets is to facilitate the efficient accommodation of the financial pressures that are bearing down on the capacities for production. The crux of the matter is that as modern-day capitalist economies grow in size and complexity, so also do the financial pressures facing their corporations and governments and what this in turn means is that these organizations must find cost-effective ways of coping with these pressures. One of these ways is by making heavy use of the capital markets. Equities are undated while bonds have finite maturities, but what all these securities have in common is that they are financial claims on the future income streams generated by producers, an observation from which it is then but a short step to the idea that what the increasing size and weight of the capital markets amounts to is the annexation of the future as an adjunct space that can take the overspill of the financial pressures of the present.[4]

In the case of private corporations, these pressures principally relate to those of market competition. In an era of rapid technological innovation and of ever intensifying competition, corporations must have constant access to large external sources of funds to finance research and product development, or to finance mergers and acquisitions, or to finance any of the other measures needed for survival. In the case of governments, the rising financial pressures on them pertain to a broader array of socio-economic changes, the most significant of which relate to demographic change. The trend rises in population ageing and in old age dependency ratios over recent decades has seen a corresponding rise in government social spending both as a percentage of GDP and as a percentage of total government expenditure.[5] While there may be scope for further tax increases, any rise in tax income would still fall far short of the sums needed to cope with the costs of financing pension and healthcare provision in addition to the costs of financing various other government expenditure commitments. Thus, it is the continually urgent need to bridge these financing gaps that explains why governments will remain major suppliers of bonds. The pressure of demographic change is also an important reason why commercial banks are among the leading issuers of bonds (classified as 'financial bonds'). Banks have traditionally relied on household deposits to fund their loans to businesses and households, but because of recent changes in household savings behaviour (households that are living longer after retirement than was previously usual are attracted by the higher yields on financial market investments), banks are having to increase their issuance of long-term bonds and short-term money market instruments to fill the gaps in the liability side of their balance sheets. Finally, as to the reasons why banks are also today heavy issuers of equities, prominent among these reasons is the tightening of the rules regarding the capital-asset ratios that banks must adhere to as safeguards against risk.

Governments play a doubly important role in driving global capital market growth because in addition to their direct quantitative contribution to the global bond supplies there is also the contribution that they make through the fact that their bonds today form the basis for an internationally unified system for pricing the risks on all financial securities. Such a system never existed in previous eras because government bond markets had never then acquired the size, depth and maturity necessary for enabling government bonds to serve in a risk benchmark capacity. All through the 19th century, and up to the 1930s, governments tended to maintain balanced budgets and only resorted to any exceptionally heavy issuance of bonds in order to finance a large-scale construction project or to meet the costs of coping with a national emergency.[6] This situation did not deter international capital flows so much as force international lenders to settle for what was conventionally considered to be a safe rate of return. The pre-First World War period that saw large capital outflows from West Europe, and from Britain in particular, illustrates the point. To quote from Ian Stone's *The Global Export of Capital from Great Britain, 1865–1914*:

> The British financial press and investing public felt that high-yielding foreign bonds were synonymous with high risk. 5–6 per cent represented a fair return on a relatively risk-free investment; securities bearing a higher

> rate of return were to be avoided. The greatest part of debentures over the half-century, both government and joint-stock company obligations, fell safely within these limits. (Stone, 1999: 31)

Government dependence on the bond markets is now both heavy and permanent for the reasons outlined here, which means that there is now always an abundance of their bonds spread across the maturity spectrum that can be used as the benchmarks for calculating and pricing the risks on corporate securities. At the same time, an internationally unified system of risk benchmarks now exists because the risk qualities of the bonds of different national governments are now themselves compared against those of the bonds of the most economically powerful government, which today is the US government. Private companies such as Standard and Poor and Moody's play a central role here because if government bonds form the basis of a globally unified system for pricing the risks on all securities, it is these companies that operationalize the system through the credit rating services that they provide to the world's institutional investors.

As observed, while governments and corporations everywhere contribute to ongoing world capital market growth, the contribution by those of the United States is larger by orders of magnitude. This disparity comes down to three key determining factors:

1. the size of the US domestic economy that sustains the ability of its government and corporations to return cash to investors;
2. the strength of the US legal and governance infrastructure that ensures the readiness of its government and corporations to return cash to investors;
3. the weight of tradition regarding US private corporations' preferred mode of external funding.

It is the first two of these factors that separates the United States from all of the EMEs, for where the United States combines a large domestic production base with a relatively strong legal and governance infrastructure, no EME currently does the same. Many EMEs are simply too small to be able to support a domestic financial market of any size, while those that do have a large domestic production base invariably have a weak governance infrastructure. China, the largest of all EMEs, illustrates the point in that while it scores fairly well as regards the quality of some public governance institutions (for example, crime prevention, public order), it continues to have a poor record as regards the quality of its private governance institutions (for example, protection of minority shareholders' rights, transparency of auditing and accounting information). It is the third of the capital market size determining factors that separates the United States from all other major advanced market economies, including those grouped together in the European Union, for while there has been a general trend growth in corporate dependence on the capital markets for the reasons outlined earlier, the pace of this growth continues to vary considerably across the advanced market economies, as exemplified by the fact that where about 80 per cent of the US corporations' external debt funding needs are met through the bond markets and only 20 per cent through bank loans, the exact reverse is true for the European Union's, UK's and Japan's corporations (SIFMA, 2022).

The United States is the world's largest supplier of financial securities, but a critical question is whether it is supplying too many securities, thus risking damage to its currency. The key consideration in this respect is the debt nature of bonds. The United States is a large supplier of equities, but it is an even larger supplier of bonds, given that the US government stands alongside US corporations among the suppliers, and the problem with this when considering the large amounts of US bonds held by foreign investors is that there may come a point when the latter abandon these bonds. The United States may still have a comparatively large production base, but the fact that its outstanding debt mountain continues to grow at a time when its percentage share of world production continues to fall also fuels a belief that the United States will eventually be unable to honour its debt commitments. To take a few early examples of this line of thinking, let us start with Martin Wolf, one of the world's most respected financial journalists. In an article published in 2004 in the *Financial Times*, Wolf stated: 'Let us be blunt about it. The US is now on the comfortable path to ruin. It is being driven along a road of ever rising deficits and debt, both external and fiscal, that risk destroying the country's credit and the global role of its currency' (Wolf, 2004). In a paper published a few years later in 2008 by two well-known international economists, Menzie Chinn and Jeffrey Frankel, the authors acknowledged the important role played by the size of US capital markets in supporting the dollar's international dominance but still went on to predict that the dollar would lose that dominance by 2015, not only because 'the euro now exists as a more serious potential rival than the mark or yen were', but also because 'the United States by now has a 25 year history of chronic current account deficits and the dollar has a 35-year history of trend depreciation' (Chinn and Frankel, 2008: 51). In a paper published a year later in 2009 by Benjamin Cohen, the doyen of international currency theorists, he similarly argued that the United States' deteriorating economic fundamentals would eventually end the dollar's dominance but without being specific about when that dominance would end, or about which rival currency would bring about that end. As he stated:

> I do not consider the persistent build-up of America's foreign debt as sustainable for long. Unless reversed by significant policy reform in Washington, the US economy's dependence on foreign capital must be expected in time to erode the advantages historically enjoyed by the greenback, creating an opportunity for challengers … the (most) plausible outcome is one in

> which the dollar's supremacy is eroded but no other single currency manages to replace it. In Jonathan Kirshner's terms, the dollar will become one of several 'peer competitors' in a fragmented currency system, with no dominant leader. (Cohen, 2009: 143)

Years have passed since this statement was made but there is no sign of the dollar becoming 'one of several peer competitors in a fragmented currency system' and a major reason for this is that foreign investors continue to pour more funds into dollar securities than into any other securities. When Chinn and Frankel predicted that the euro would challenge the dollar as the world's dominant currency by 2015, their central argument was that the United States' 'chronic' deficits meant that it could not 'count on being bailed out indefinitely' (Chin and Frankel, 2008: 67). A similar position was advanced a decade later by Eswar Prasad. In a book published in 2014, Prasad had shown how the Federal Reserve's central bank swap lines and other US post-crisis policy initiatives had helped to tighten the dollar's grip on the global financial system (Prasad, 2014). Yet, in an opinion article published in the *Financial Times* four years later in the midst of Donald Trump's presidency titled 'America beware: dollar supremacy is not forever', Prasad warned that Trump's heavy and indiscriminate use of the dollar as an economic and political weapon might eventually hurt the dollar by 'eroding foreign investors' trust and confidence in the US and its institutions' (Prasad, 2018). The idea that is implicit in these arguments, that to protect the dollar the United States has to count on being 'bailed out' by its foreign investors or that it cannot afford to 'erode' foreign investors' trust and confidence in its institutions, is that the United States has really nothing of value to give back to these investors in return for their goodwill, that, to put it another way, there is ultimately nothing of real substance underpinning the US dollar's dominance. This idea was made explicit in an article by James Galbraith published in May 2022, when he argued that:

> [U]p to now the dollar-based order has been supported mainly by instability elsewhere and the lack of a credible alternative or compelling reason to create one, or where such reasons are felt, the ability to do so. … The system has been held up, in short, by confidence in itself, and not, so far as one can see, by much of anything else. (Galbraith, 2022: np)

Now, if there is not 'much of anything' underpinning the dollar's attraction for foreign investors, one is then hard put to explain why these investors have carried on pouring substantial sums into dollar securities. In 2004, when Martin Wolf penned his article warning that America was on the comfortable path to ruin, foreign investors held about \$6.2 trillion worth of US securities. By 2008, that figure had grown to about \$8.9 trillion, by 2018 it had grown to \$17.6 trillion, and by 2022 it had grown to \$23.2 trillion (SIFMA, 2023). These figures clearly show that there is something seriously wrong with the current conceptualizations of the financial foundations of dollar dominance, and that something is a category error at the heart of all current macroeconomic theories.

The error is that these theories continue to take the household saver to be the representative investor on the demand side of the financial markets when the reality is that it is the large institutional investor that is now the dominant type of investor. While institutional investors include sovereign wealth funds, hedge funds and high net worth individuals, the largest group when taken collectively are the asset managers, the pension and mutual funds and insurance companies. For long a small cottage industry catering for the very wealthy, asset management has become in many countries a mass industry catering for the retirement and other welfare arrangements of large sections of the population. With this growth in asset management scale has come a corresponding growth in the need for assets in which clients' monies can be stored and from which monies can be extracted to pay clients. Although there are other types of assets that serve as stores of value for asset managers, including cash, real estate, gold and other material commodities, financial securities necessarily comprise the majority proportion of their portfolios because what sets them apart from other asset classes is their ability to combine a large value storage property (because they are available in abundance) with relatively high liquidity (defined here as ease of trading with minimal impact on price) and portability (securities can be traded away from their initial conditions of issuance unlike, say, bank credit loans). The one notable difference separating asset managers is that where the mutual funds tend to weight their portfolios towards equities, the insurance companies, and also to an extent pension funds, who roughly know the amounts of funds that have to be periodically paid out, tend to give greater weight to bonds as their finite maturities make them more suitable for duration matching purposes. This difference aside, the main point is that a substantial volume of demand for corporate and government securities is ensured, and that this volume demand will remain permanent given that the economic costs of population ageing will likely force governments to increasingly shift away from universal welfare provision towards more selective forms, thus forcing increasing numbers of households to enlist the services of asset managers when making their own private welfare arrangements.

While the large size of institutional asset managers' demand capacity for securities is to the benefit of security issuing organizations, the obverse side of this demand capacity is that it is exercised on condition that borrowers adhere to an array of new transparency and information standards on the one hand and to an array of new governance standards on the other whose combined effects are to restrict discretion over cash disbursements to investors. The rationale behind this restriction is that as it is only through their prices that securities can acquire a quantitative value storage capacity, and as these prices are nothing other than the discounted values of expected future cash returns, it follows that they can only remain solid enough to preserve a determinate quantity of value over time on condition that cash returns are made at a certain rate and with a certain regularity. The rationale behind the subjection of security issuers to two distinct sets of behavioural standards is that where conformity with transparency and information standards allow investors to accurately assess the financial health of corporations and governments and hence their *ability* to return cash, conformity with governance standards help to ensure a *readiness* to return cash. Broadly put, the governance of organizations concerns how they conduct their affairs to meet the different priorities of their various stakeholders, but for institutional investors the question of good governance ultimately comes down to the level of priority given to their interests as outside investors: high priority means that there is a reasonably good guarantee that cash will be returned to them in the required amounts and at the required intervals, whereas a low priority means that there is no guarantee that cash will be returned. The question of shareholder primacy in the matter of corporate governance is of particular importance here, for where bonds pay interest by law and thus already have some backing guarantee of value storage capacity, equities pay dividends on discretion, which means that to give corporate managers too much discretion over cash returns is to risk undermining, if not completely negating, the value storage capacity of equities.

If current macroeconomic theories continue to take the household saver to be the representative investor despite these well-known facts, it is ultimately because the differences that separate households from institutional investors are not considered to be fundamental. Asset managers may have more professional expertise, or they can, on account of their large size, wield more market power over security issuers, but these differences are nevertheless held to be secondary to what all investors have in common, which is that as lenders of funds they have cause to view financial securities differently to the way that they are viewed by those borrowing funds. For corporations and governments that use securities as funding instruments, it is only their 'flow' dimension that is important: they raise funds at one point on the promise to return a stream of interest payments or dividends before repaying the funds at a future point and, in the meantime, they use the funds to finance various expenditures. For investors who use securities as 'investables', it is both their 'flow' and 'stock' dimensions that are important: they buy securities at one point on the expectation of receiving a stream of payments before being finally repaid at another point and, in the meantime, they use the securities as stores of value. Now, when securities markets are only viewed from a perspective that divides all participating agents according to whether they are either sellers or buyers of securities, then it would appear that there is no harm in assuming that all investors can be collapsed into the same single category of the representative household. This assumption is completely wrong. It is wrong because the differences separating institutional investors from household savers are now fundamental, differences of kind rather than of degree, and the reason for this lies in the distinction between holding financial securities as a matter of *choice* and holding financial securities as a matter of *necessity*. Households may well invest their savings in securities should the returns on them look more favourable than are those on alternative asset classes such as real estate but should the returns on these alternative assets turn out to be more favourable there is absolutely nothing in their function as households that prevents them from switching all of their savings to these assets. It therefore follows that if security issuers were never in the past tied to such tight behavioural rules and constraints as exist today, it was not only because households who were then the dominant type of investors lacked sufficient market power to enforce such rules and constraints but also because they lacked sufficiently strong motivation. The situation is very different for today's institutional asset managers. They can hold cash for liquidity purposes, and they can hold real estate assets for higher return purposes, but the exigencies of their role as financial intermediaries require them at all times to hold the bulk of their asset portfolios in the form of financial securities, assets that combine large value storage capacity with liquidity and, as we say, it is this requirement that explains why it has been institutional investors that have forced into existence new financial market rules of behaviour such as can help solidify the prices and hence value storage capacities of financial securities.

Returning now to the question of whether foreign investors can abandon dollar securities on the scale necessary to hurt the dollar, the answer can of course be affirmative if the question is approached from a theoretical standpoint that takes the household to be the representative investor, for just as households are always free to abandon financial securities in favour of other asset classes, so are foreign investors always free to abandon dollar securities in favour of other assets. On the contrary, the answer has to be negative if the question is approached from a standpoint that takes the representative investor to be one for whom the holding of financial securities is a binding necessity for what then becomes clear is that foreign investors are not free to abandon dollar securities on any large scale. One factor that closes down this freedom is the lack of alternative supplies of non-dollar financial securities available for use as safe stores of value, but a more crucial – because more compelling – factor is the sheer strength of the dollar's gravitational pull on the world's institutional investors. It may not have been part of institutional asset managers' intention to help bolster the foundations of dollar dominance in the modern era when forcing new rules of financial market behaviour into existence, but this has precisely been the result of this enforcement due to the radical transformation undergone by financial securities on the back of the new rules. Absent these rules and equities and bonds are always in danger of remaining mere promissory notes, but with their imposition equities and bonds become genuinely safe stores of value. From being particles without matter, securities become particles filled with matter and what this means is that when all the securities of a country's organizations are aggregated together, this aggregation gives that country's capital markets mass and a corresponding power of attraction for investors: the greater the mass, the greater the power of attraction, and no country's markets have greater mass and power of attraction than those of the United States. The United States on its own currently accounts for around 40 per cent of world equity and bond volumes, while other advanced market economy countries account for around 45 per cent and the EME group account for the remaining 15 per cent. Large as they are, these financial market size disparities become far larger still when translated into currency terms for where the United States' securities volumes comprise a single, same currency mass of dollar securities, those of the other countries shrink considerably when priced in their local currencies. These size disparities may not be a matter of great concern for countries outside of the United States were there to be strict controls on international portfolio flows. However, as there are few such controls in place, these flows are very much a matter of concern and they are so because they entail a highly uneven distribution of gains and losses, with the United States reaping the gains and other countries, most notably the EMEs, incurring the losses.

These gains and losses basically take on two forms, one pecuniary-related and the other policy-related. The source of the pecuniary-related form is the correlation between the risks on securities and the corresponding yield premiums that must be factored into their prices: the higher the risks, the higher the yield premiums. To illustrate the point, consider the US capital markets. These are by far the largest and deepest in the world, and as such they are highly attractive to foreign investors in that not only is there an abundance of securities in which to store their funds, but also a wide choice range of different security types across which they can move funds without restriction according to economic circumstances. However, these advantages to foreign investors must be paid for in the sense that they will on average earn comparatively low returns on their dollar assets. Thus, for example, they will earn no currency risk premium (due to the range of choice of US dollar securities across which investments can be moved according to any change in economic conditions without being subject to exchange rate frictions); low credit risk premiums (due to the general strength and reputation of the US legal and governance infrastructure); low liquidity risk premiums (due to the depth of the US capital markets and hence the ease of trading with minimal price impact); and a low sovereign risk premium (due to the scale of US domestic economic activity and hence the corresponding government power of taxation). By contrast, foreign investors can on average earn comparatively high returns on investments in countries that host small local currency-denominated capital markets because in these cases there will be currency risk premiums (any cross-security flows generated by any change in economic conditions will also typically take on a cross-currency dimension), high credit risk premiums (that may reflect a weak legal and governance infrastructure as much as a small domestic production base for local corporations) and high sovereign risk premiums (reflective of small domestic tax bases whose smallness may again be the result of a small domestic economy as also of a weak legal infrastructure). It is testimony to just how wide is the gap separating the yields paid out on US securities and the yields paid out on foreign securities that, year in and year out, the US extracts far greater sums of monies from foreign countries than it pays out even while the total amounts of foreign investments in US securities are far greater than the total amounts of US holdings of foreign securities.[7] Foreign investors are not earning less than are the US-based investors because they are somehow less experienced or less astute than are their US counterparts when it comes to overseas portfolio investments. Rather, the main cause of this anomaly lies in the way that US asset managers are able to take advantage of the size asymmetries separating the dollar financial markets from those of other small currency markets, most notably those located in the EMEs. Even if certain EME-based organizations have exactly the same governance and economic performance records as do their US counterparts, they would still have to pay out higher risk premiums on their securities simply because of the small size and peripheral position of their domestic financial markets.

The source of the policy-related form of the gains and losses resulting from cross-border portfolio flows lies in the correlation between capital market size and the extent to which exchange rate volatility is factored into the conduct of monetary policy. Let us again start with the United States, which has the largest and deepest capital markets. Any fluctuation in the dollar's international value will have a differential economic impact on the United States' exporting and importing firms, an impact that then sets in train portfolio investment shifts across US financial securities with monies flowing into the securities of firms that have benefited from the dollar's fluctuation and out of the securities of firms that have been adversely affected. As these investment shifts occur within the same dollar-denominated mass of securities they do not further aggravate the fluctuation in the dollar's value, thus limiting its negative effects on the underlying real economy. It is this fact, that the large mass of financial securities behind the US dollar acts as a currency shock-absorber, that explains why the US monetary authorities can treat the dollar's international value with 'benign neglect', a fact which in turn explains why they can conduct their domestic monetary policy without reference to the monetary policy of any other country. By contrast, everything is reversed in countries with small capital markets. Any investment shifts across securities triggered by the impact of any exchange rate change on exporting or importing firms will likely also take the form of cross-currency shifts that will in turn amplify the initial exchange rate change and hence its effects on the underlying real economy. Thus, policy makers in countries with small capital markets, the very smallness of which can cause them to be currency shock amplifiers, do not have the luxury of treating their currencies' international value with benign neglect. On the contrary, that value must be fixed against the currency most heavily used in an international role, namely, the dollar, which not only means that policy makers must keep an eye on US monetary policy but also that substantial dollar reserves be held for currency market intervention purposes.

A major conclusion that falls out of this discussion is that if equities and bonds constitute the solid matter of the financial markets through which countries with small financial markets are held subject to the gravitational pull of the large US dollar market, the pecuniary and policy related consequences of that gravitational pull are such as to have the reverse effect of further compounding those financial market size asymmetries. We say that foreign portfolio investors and foreign central banks are drawn to US corporate and government securities markets because these are the world's largest, deepest and most liquid, but in being so drawn to these markets they then contribute to their further growth in size, depth and liquidity, thus contributing to the ease with which US corporations and federal government can issue substantially more securities before coming up against repayment constraints. The large mass of dollar securities therefore continually begets an even greater mass as foreign institutional investors are continually willing to trade low returns on their dollar assets off against the various benefits accruing from these assets, thereby enabling the United States to continually issue increasing amounts of securities on an affordable basis. By contrast, a small mass of local currency-denominated securities produced by a country perpetuates continuing smallness as foreign portfolio investors holding these securities demand such high returns as compensation for the various risks attaching to them as will seriously constrain the amounts of securities that can be safely issued by the country's organizations. International portfolio flows therefore ultimately serve not only as the medium through which the large dollar financial markets control small financial markets through their gravitational pull but also as the medium that ensures that the respective sizes of these markets, and hence the respective positions of controller and controlled, lock together in a mutually reinforcing dynamic.

The upshot is that dollar dominance looks secure for the foreseeable future. For any prediction to the contrary to be possible, one must suppose that the financialization of capitalism can somehow be reversed so that the world's securities markets are again scaled down to a size approximating that for annual world output. In such a world, where a national currency's international standing would again be ultimately determined by the issuing country's underlying economic fundamentals, one could plausibly conjecture that other currencies will do to the dollar in the present century what the dollar did to the pound sterling in the last century. That world, however, has gone and it will not return. Having just begun, the financialization of capitalism will continue to unfold because, apart from the need to facilitate the efficient allocation and deployment of resources, the widening scale asymmetry separating the world's securities markets from world GDP is being driven by the need to accommodate the financial pressures bearing down on corporations and governments, and these pressures will continue to grow in line with the continuing growth in the size and complexity of modern-day economies. On the other side of the equation, many of the pressures behind the increasing rate of supply of financial securities are also those that lie behind the increasing rate of institutional investor demand for them for use as stores of value. The problem is that these investors' insistence that security issuers comply with such conditions as can consolidate their securities' value storage capacities means that not all borrowing organizations across all countries benefit equally from having institutional investors on the demand side of the securities markets. On the contrary, those borrowing organizations situated in countries that best combine a large production base with a strong legal and governance infrastructure benefit disproportionately more, and this above all means the organizations based in the United States. Taking full advantage of the rise in global institutional investor demand for bonds and equities over recent decades, the US government and private corporations have led the way in increasing the volume supplies of these securities to unprecedented heights. In so doing, they may not have consciously aimed at reinforcing the US dollar's international dominance. This result, however, has been precisely that which has been secured by the build-up of the US capital markets to the point of supplying the dollar with enough backing mass as to make it the centre of gravity in the international financial system. The global trade and production realms may now be characterized, as is so frequently done, by fragmentation and a scattering apart of countries as those in the East gain in ascendency and vie with those in the West, but no such characterization can be applied to the global financial realm where the dense mass of dollar securities keeps virtually all other financial markets trapped in its gravitational field. If any country or region can hope to have its currency resist the gravitational pull of the dollar, let alone hope to have it challenge the dollar as the world's top international currency, it too must expand its financial markets to the extent necessary to making its currency a centre of gravity in its own right. This is the lesson that had to be learned the hard way by the countries that formed the euro in 1999.

TWO

Resisting the Dollar's Gravitational Force: The Euro's Rationale Revisited

The majority expert opinion at the euro's launch in 1999 was that this currency was a quintessentially political construction.[1] Any differences within this opinion were over particulars. One line of argument, for example, held that the euro was designed to enable France and Germany to consolidate their continental ambitions, the former being able to achieve a parity with Germany in the conduct of European monetary policy that it did not have in the European Monetary System (EMS) and the latter being able to benefit from a currency union that, by linking Germany with France and other European Union (EU) countries closer together, would make future wars impossible.[2] Another line of argument was that the French, together with certain other European governing elites, would find it easier to realize their geo-political ambitions by joining their national currencies into a single large currency that could then seriously challenge the US dollar's hegemonic position at the top of the global currency pyramid.[3] Either way, what was common to both lines of argument was the conviction that any economic considerations behind the creation of the euro were lost to political objectives.

The key development that helped to reinforce this conclusion was the size of the euro area at the time of its launch. Had the euro's planners kept to the strictures of optimum currency area (OCA) theory or kept to their own criteria as laid down in the Maastricht Treaty, then no more than six or seven of the EU applicant countries would have been eligible for euro entry. Yet virtually all the applicant countries were invited to join the euro regardless of the fact that many of them were nowhere near meeting the necessary entry conditions however these were formulated. The large size of the new currency union drew warnings from many leading economists and other academics that this size would pose severe problems, with some commentators going so far as to doubt whether the euro would survive at all. These warnings became fewer in number and softer in tone during the euro's first years of existence when its member countries registered reasonable growth rates, but they then resurfaced on a much louder basis when the financial crisis of 2007–8 spread to the eurozone as a whole in 2009. Indeed, as far as many experts on European political economy were concerned, the eurozone's crisis originated from the fact that the decision to go for a large euro was motivated entirely by political considerations. Paul De Grauwe, for example, stated that:

> The Eurozone's present state of crisis originated from decisions made at its creation. The decision to create a monetary union was motivated by political objectives and completely disregarded the economics of a monetary union. Political leaders did not understand the necessary economic conditions for a successful monetary union and did not recognise the inherent fragility of the monetary union they established. (De Grauwe, 2013b: 1)

In what follows we shall put the contrary argument that Europe's political leaders did understand the necessary economic conditions for a monetary union and did recognize the inherent fragility of a large monetary union project even while going ahead with it. What will be central to this argument is the premise that a monetary union in the contemporary era of financialization serves two distinct economic functions: on the one hand, an internal, efficiency-enhancing function in the sense that such a union between countries eliminates exchange rate volatility as a key impediment to their closer trade and production integration and, on the other hand, an external, protection enhancing function in the sense that monetary union provides a sheltering hub both against global financial pressures in general and against the gravitational force of the dollar in particular. The dilemma that faced the architects of the eurozone is that these two distinctive functions of monetary union pull in completely opposite directions as regards its optimum size, for where the internal efficiency-enhancing function is served the better the *smaller* is the number of the member countries of the union, the external protection enhancing function is served the better the *larger* is the number of member countries. By the late 1990s, the euro's creators chose to resolve this dilemma by opting for a large eurozone, but that it was by no means an easy choice is evidenced by the fact that for the most part of this decade the euro's creators continued to plan for a small eurozone as dictated by the criteria for eurozone membership first set down in the European Commission's 1990 document, *One Market One Money* (OMOM).

That document gave close consideration to the theory of OCA, according to which the benefits to countries joining a currency union will not be offset by the loss of national control over monetary and exchange rate policy providing that three major conditions are met:

1. that there are no barriers to the free movement of labour within the union (the 'labour mobility' criterion);
2. that the member countries must be open and trade extensively with each other (the 'openness' criterion); and
3. that the member countries' production and export bases must be widely diversified (the 'product differentiation' criterion).

Although mindful of the OCA theory's criteria for a successful currency union, the euro's planners chose to disregard them in favour of an alternative set of criteria (subsequently ratified in the Treaty of Maastricht agreed in December 1991) that instead put the emphasis on the monetary variables of inflation and interest rates on the one hand (specifically, a candidate country's inflation and central interest rate should not be more than 2 per cent higher than the average rates registered by the best three performing candidate countries) and the fiscal variables of deficit and debt to gross domestic product (GDP) ratios on the other (specifically, a country's annual budget deficit should not be more than 3 per cent of its GDP and its national debt should not be more than 60 per cent of its GDP). This switch in emphasis on euro membership criteria did nothing to alter the matter of its optimal size. A strict enforcement of the OCA-type convergence criteria would have meant that only about five to seven EU countries, principally those drawn from the northern part of the EU, would have been able to join the euro in 1999 because only this group of countries had identifiably similar economic structures. However, the same result would have followed from a strict enforcement of the Maastricht convergence criteria because only a handful of countries had by then fully complied with these criteria or were close to complying with them. Yet, what actually happened is that the criteria were sufficiently relaxed as to allow virtually every EU applicant country to join the euro, an event that, as we say, was widely taken as conclusive proof that the euro was a one-sidedly political project.

To understand the sudden change of position regarding the eurozone's size at its launch in 1999 we first need to understand that what set the 1990s apart from the two previous decades was the new, and highly lethal, combination of capital mobility with capital market volume. The 1970s may have marked the start of global capital mobility following the break-up of the post-war Bretton Woods system in 1971, but it was still a decade of relatively low capital market volume as attested by the previously cited fact that the nominal value of global securities stocks in 1980 amounted to just $11 trillion, a sum roughly on a par with the nominal value of world GDP in that year. Even as late as 1990, the global nominal value of securities stocks was still only slightly larger than that for world GDP ($22 trillion versus $19 trillion). But from that point on, the rate of growth of global securities stocks began to significantly outstrip that of world GDP so that by 1995 their nominal value of $45 trillion was one and a half times the $30 trillion figure for world GDP and by 2000 their nominal value of $82 trillion was more than two and a half times the $33 trillion figure for world GDP. The world's large institutional investors would have welcomed the growth of securities stocks because it represented a growth in the supply of portable stores of value, but the flip side of this development was that it provided hedge funds and other speculative vehicles with massive financial fire power when targeting particular national currencies that were perceived to be vulnerable. As was pointed out in a Group of Ten report published in 1993: 'the growth in the size, integration and agility of international financial markets has greatly increased the scale of pressure that can be exerted against an exchange rate when market sentiment shifts' (Group of Ten, 1993: 33). Europe felt the scale of pressure that can be exerted against exchange rates in the summer of 1992 with the EMS crisis, but if there was then any lingering doubt as to whether this type of pressure was likely to be temporary rather than permanent in nature, that doubt was removed by the Asian currency crisis that broke out in the summer of 1997. It was about then that the European Commission started to give greater priority to the euro's role as a protective hub against global financial pressures and hence to start thinking of a large rather than a small euro area from the outset.

What drove the Commission's change of position regarding the size of the eurozone was its change of thinking regarding the relation between the closer European capital market integration made possible by currency integration on the one hand and the role played by European and foreign institutional investors on the other. In the early 1990s the Commission's emphasis was how institutional investors could help to promote the efficiency-enhancing benefits of currency and capital market integration by dropping their demands for exchange rate risk premiums, thereby helping to reduce European corporations' borrowing costs. As was stated in the 1990 OMOM document, in the absence of a common currency 'agents would still form expectations of exchange rate changes and/or ask for risk premiums when they lend in a foreign currency, with the consequence that real interest rates differ across the Community and that cross-country financing is limited by the exchange rate risk' (European Commission, 1990: 33). Further on in that same document the Commission observed that institutional investors could help promote the international weight and standing of a new European currency by their readiness to increase their holdings of the new currency-denominated securities. To quote from OMOM:

> The creation of EMU would give rise to a specific effect: it would lead private agents to increase their demand for ecu denominated assets in order to reweight their transaction balances and to achieve a more balanced distribution of their portfolios between the major currencies of the three major economic zones. It is often argued by financial market participants that no real alternative to the dollar exists at present since the size, liquidity and depth of European and Japanese markets are still very inferior to those of the US market. As this would no longer hold as EMU with a single currency triggers the unification of European markets, a move towards the ecu can be expected. (European Commission, 1990: 188)

Despite the fact that the Commission recognized that an integrated European capital market would enhance the European Community's weight in the international arena in addition to enhancing economic efficiency inside the Community, it still saw the latter goal as having overriding priority. To again quote from OMOM: 'The primary economic aim of EMU is to strengthen the integration of the Community and to improve its economic performance. However, due to the Community's weight EMU will also have far-reaching implications for the world's economy' (European Commission, 1990: 178).

By the later part of the 1990s, the Commission's position had palpably shifted in that it was by now attaching the same priority to the external weight-enhancing effects of economic and monetary union (EMU) and European capital market integration as to their internal efficiency-enhancing effects. Clear evidence of this shift was provided in a Commission document published in July of 1997, *External Aspects of Economic and Monetary Union*. The document had been prepared by a committee chaired by Yves-Thibault de Silguy, Commissioner responsible for economic, monetary and financial affairs. In a speech given in Hong Kong in September 1997 where de Silguy summarized the main conclusions of the document, he began by emphasizing how the euro would give Europe a presence in the international monetary system: 'Europe is the world's number one economic and commercial power but has no presence on the international monetary scene. The arrival of the euro will correct this paradox, opening the way to a more balanced multi-polar international monetary system' (de Silguy, 1997: 6). While the euro would help achieve the goal of multipolarity, de Silguy made clear that in addition to the combined strength of the European production and trading systems, the combined size of the European financial markets would also be key to securing that goal:

> [T]he euro will be a major currency alongside the dollar and the yen. The euro has a potential home market of 370 million consumers. It will be based on a vast and highly liquid financial market. Progressively, the euro is likely to take on a major role as an invoicing currency, a reserve currency and a currency used for

> the diversification of international portfolios. (de Silguy, 1997: 7)

This latter point regarding the attraction of an integrated European capital for international investors was raised in the 1990 OMOM document, but in de Silguy's speech it is given repeated emphasis. Thus, he stated that once the European Central Bank begins to implement monetary policy in euro and once European governments and corporations begin to issue euro-denominated debt and equity: 'all this implies that interbank, money and capital markets will switch quickly to the euro. In this way, the euro will provide a credible alternative to the dollar for international investors, particularly those in Asian and far eastern markets' (de Silguy, 1997: 7). Further on in his speech, de Silguy again stated:

> The creation of a unified and liquid European capital market will make it easier for Asian investors, both public and private, to diversify their holdings. This is a natural continuation of an on-going trend. The euro will be an attractive currency for Asian investors because of the stability-oriented policy mix of the euro area and because of the liquidity, size and transparency of markets for euro-denominated assets. (de Silguy, 1997: 7)

The hope behind de Silguy's emphasis on the attractions of a large and liquid euro capital market was not only that foreign investors would increase their holdings of euro assets but that they would also withdraw some of their funds from dollar assets in order to do so. These two developments taken together would bring the euro capital markets closer in size to those of the dollar markets, thus enabling European monetary authorities to discount the effects of any changes in the euro–dollar exchange rate, which would in turn enable them to operate policies independently of the policies pursued by the US monetary authorities. Recall from the previous section that it is the large mass of dollar-denominated securities that allows the US authorities to conduct their monetary policies solely with reference to their internal priorities and without regard for the repercussions of those policies on the dollar's international value. Recall also that any gyrations in that value can be a source of great instability in other currency areas with small financial markets, the upshot of this point being that only by building up a large currency-denominated financial market can a currency area cope with the pressures of the dollar. That this same logic was central to de Silguy's thinking when stating that the 'progressive development of the euro will help create a better balanced international monetary system' is made clear in the passage that immediately followed this statement:

> The world is today dominated by the US dollar which is used for 50% of commercial transactions and 80% of operations on financial markets. This structural imbalance in the international monetary system is a factor of instability. The US domestic economy is highly protected against the effects of fluctuations in the external value of the dollar. American policy makers are naturally more concerned by the internal effects of their actions than the potential impact on the international monetary system. The result is that the world economy is heavily exposed to the effects of often significant and unpredictable movements in the value of the dollar. (de Silguy, 1997: 7)

We can now see why the Commission's eventual decision to push for a large euro area made complete economic sense. As the Commission in its 1990 OMOM document still accorded priority to the euro's internal efficiency-enhancing role, it was at that time reluctant to go for a large euro area from the start because it still believed that the costs of such of an action would outweigh the benefits. However, when by the late 1990s the Commission began to give equal priority to the euro's external, international weight-enhancing role, it accordingly began to see that the benefits of a large euro area would outweigh the costs. De Silguy spoke of the benefits of a 'balanced' international monetary system, but 'symmetry' was another operative word used in the Commission's document of 1997: 'EMU should increase the symmetry in the international monetary system, thereby enhancing the benefits and allowing for a more efficient distribution of the benefits derived from international economic coordination' (European Commission, 1997: 2). The Commission continued to formally stress the need for euro applicant countries to meet the Maastricht convergence criteria, but the logic of their ambition to make the euro a serious alternative to the dollar as a centre of gravity in the international monetary system militated towards relaxing those entry criteria. This relaxation was duly done in May 1998, when the decision was taken to allow 11 of the 12 EU applicant countries to join the euro at its launch in 1999 (Greece eventually joined in 2002).

While the changing global economic and financial landscape gave context and urgency to the need for a large euro area it was the countervailing tensions between the differing policy priorities of Germany, Italy and France that provided the dynamic impulse behind the eventual creation of such an area. In elaborating on this point, we begin by looking at Germany's position. The fundamental tenets of Germany's post-war macroeconomic policy were, first, that its principal objective should be the control of domestic inflation and, second, that this objective be achieved through fiscal rectitude rather than through manipulation of the currency's international exchange rate. It was the rigid adherence to these two tenets that helped to precipitate the EMS crisis of 1992 in that it was the conflict between, on the one hand, Germany's insistence on maintaining a high interest rate to contain the inflationary pressures arising out of German unification and, on the other hand, Britain's and other EMS member countries' demand that monetary policy be loosened to help them cope with the deflationary pressures emanating from

North America that gave hedge funds and other speculative vehicles the opportunity to bet heavily against many of the EMS currencies. The cardinal lesson that Germany took from the crisis was that at fault was not its policy of prioritizing price stability at any cost, but the flawed structure of the EMS as a 'system of fixed but adjustable exchange rates, which [has been] accurately called "half-baked" because adjustments never take place at the right moment' (Pöhl, 1995: 67). Thus, while Germany still took the position that a single European currency was the preferred alternative to the EMS, unlike Britain that took the opposite position that a return to freely floating national currencies was the better option, it also held strongly to the view that internal price stability within the new eurozone should take priority over the euro's exchange rate stability. As Karl Otto Pöhl, Chairman of the Bundesbank from 1980 to 1991, declared: 'the mandate of the ECB must be to maintain stability of the value of money as the prime objective of European monetary policy. ... Domestic stability of the value of money must take precedence over exchange-rate stability' (Pöhl, 1995: 109). Given Germany's rigid adherence to the view that price stability should be achieved through fiscal discipline and given that Italy's and other so-called 'Club Med' countries' record on this score was poor, to say the least, one could understand the Bundesbank's preference for an initially small euro area composed solely of countries that met the strict entry criteria. As Pöhl stated, participation in the common currency:

> should be strictly limited to members that offer adequate assurance that their inflation rate, fiscal deficit, and public debt, as well as other relevant factors, will not be causes of discord and tension from the beginning. I have long favoured a multiple speed approach that would allow a core group to move ahead fully confident of success, while allowing others to join as they meet the necessary entry criteria. (Pöhl, 1995: 96)

While the majority of the EMS member countries opted to move towards a single currency, in contrast to the UK's position of reverting to freely floating national currencies, the country that most typified that majority's rationale for wanting a single currency was not Germany, but Italy. The EMS crisis of 1992 produced diverse reactions among the EMS member states, but the general stance as exemplified by Italy was that in a world of newly freed capital movements, the single currency was the only way to achieve currency stability. In effect, Italy's order of policy priorities was the exact opposite of that of Germany's: where Germany saw the prioritization of price stability as a means of guaranteeing exchange rate stability, the weakness of Italy's domestic socio-economic structures and governance institutions meant that Italy saw the prioritization of exchange rate stability as a means of guaranteeing price stability. While this conflict of priorities could be more or less reconciled during the 1980s following the establishment of the EMS in 1979, that reconciliation ended abruptly following German reunification. When the Italian and other central banks called for an orchestrated response to the speculative attacks on EMS currencies occasioned by the emergence of serious policy disagreements between the member countries, the Bundesbank refused to oblige and change its policy stance accordingly. This was despite the stark warning of the consequences of the Bundesbank's intransigence given by Carlo Azeglio Ciampi, the then Governor of the Banca d'Italia, at an unofficial meeting between finance ministers and central bank governors held in Paris in August 1992: 'Let nobody be deceived that he can save himself by acting alone: if we act in isolation, all today's weak currencies will end up like the Curiatii.'[4] So desperate was Romano Prodi's government to return to a situation where exchange rate stability could compensate for the lack of stability in the other determinants of inflation, that it did everything in its power to ensure not only that Italy re-join the EMS, which it did in November 1996, but that it would be among the first wave of countries to join the euro. Although in the years between 1993 and 1998 Italy did move towards the convergence criteria as laid down in the Maastricht Treaty and as subsequently reinforced by the Stability and Growth Pact that was formally ratified in May 1997, it nevertheless fell short of a number of those criteria in May 1998, the date at which it would be decided which applicant countries would be invited to join the euro. Despite this fact, and despite Germany's known opposition to any relaxation of any of the convergence criteria, Italy was invited, as were Spain and several other countries that similarly fell short of several of the criteria. The explanation for this turn of events lay with France.

The Bundesbank's views on pressing ahead with EMU with an initially small group of countries were strongly opposed by the French government. Michele Fratianni, reviewing the controversy over the 'maxi versus mini EMU' issue, observed that:

> [T]he deflationary impact of the convergence criteria and the consequent swing to the left of the electorate, especially in France, made Italy's entry to Stage III more acceptable. The new Socialist government in France was willing to make the case for Italy's entry in Stage III; and so was Austria. Opposition to Italy was withering as was the opposition to a maxi EMU. (Fratianni, 1998: 383)

The reason why this opposition was withering was not only political in that a single currency limited to Germany's northern European allies and that excluded Italy, a close European ally of France, would dangerously limit France's clout. There was also an equally strong economic reason in that France had major trading ties with Italy and Spain and thus to leave these countries out of the new single currency would effectively give them a competitive edge by allowing them the option of devaluation. In the event that these countries were excluded from EMU, France could of course still maintain its competitive position were the European Central Bank (ECB)'s mandate broadened to include exchange rate targeting in its list of priorities. It was this possibility that the French would indeed push for such a broadening of the ECB's mandate in the event that the southern European countries were left out of the new single currency that compelled the Bundesbank to drop its opposition to the latter's inclusion. The dilemma facing the Bundesbank was stark: either the French would have to be left out of EMU so as to safeguard the ECB's independence from political interference, or, if France were to be included in EMU, then so would Italy and other southern European countries also have to be included if the ECB's independence was to be preserved. Given that France's exclusion from EMU was absolutely unthinkable, the Franco-German axis having been at the core of the whole European Union project from its outset, the Bundesbank had no choice but to accede to France's demand for an enlarged EMU.

In 2009 the eurozone went into a deep crisis from which it did not emerge until about 2014/15. In a later part of this book, we shall outline the reasons why the eurozone countries, in common with other non-euro European countries such as the UK, were so profoundly impacted by the repercussions of the great financial crisis of 2007–8 that originated in the United States. For the present we note that the eurozone's crisis served to expose the structural flaws in its architecture, chief of which was the absence of a political/fiscal union to match currency union. Given that there was no system of fiscal transfers within the eurozone and given that its inclusion of so many countries with differing economic profiles was bound to make it prone to a severe asymmetric shock as occurred following the outbreak of the financial crisis in 2007–8, the eurozone's future as an integrated operational totality looked for a while to hang in the balance. What further helped to make the eurozone's situation particularly dangerous was the post-crisis policy stance taken by its most powerful member country, Germany. The latter had accepted the necessity for the eurozone's governments' debt-financed bailouts of their banking systems, but no sooner had this task been achieved than Germany insisted on a coordinated switch to austerity policies aimed at bringing government debt to GDP ratios back to their pre-crisis levels. As this switch to austerity was certain to further accentuate the economic difficulties already being faced by many of the eurozone member countries, the question that inevitably arose was whether it might be better to break up the eurozone so as to allow its ex-member countries to pursue their own independent post-crisis policies. In this context, the rationale behind a large eurozone became a matter of some importance: if the large eurozone at the point of its creation had an economic rationale, then its break-up would likely be more costly than beneficial to its member countries while the reverse would be the case if the large eurozone was from the outset a political project that had no justifiable economic rationale.

This latter position was that taken by many economists on both the heterodox and mainstream wings of the profession. On the heterodox wing, Heiner Flassbeck and Costas Lapavitsas were among the most vocal advocates of the euro's break-up. According to their view as this was put in 2015, the euro 'is the money of an alliance of unequal sovereign states riven with hierarchical relations with Germany at the top' and, as a German-dominated euro is a currency that is 'currently strangling the European economy', the only 'realistic progressive option would be to return to national currencies, thus facilitating recovery of economic independence, defence of democracy and protection of national sovereignty' (Flassbeck and Lapavitsas, 2015: 86). The equation that was drawn here between national control over a currency and national control over economic policy does not tally with the experience of most of those countries that retain their own currencies while also struggling to survive in today's financialized global economy. On the contrary, the need to closely tie their currencies to a major international currency such as the dollar or the euro in order to minimize the impact of exchange rate volatility on their domestic economies requires these countries to closely align their monetary policies with those pursued in the United States or in the eurozone. In other words, the correct lesson that had to be drawn from international experience is that any country that exited a German-dominated euro would not have reclaimed national sovereignty over the control of monetary policy so much as go from having a small share in the exercise of policy control to having no policy control. In this event, euro exit would have made it more, not less, difficult to implement the kind of expansionist policies needed to promote domestic economic growth in the wake of the eurozone's crisis.

Recognizing this danger, Joseph Stiglitz, a major mainstream economist and Nobel Laureate, argued that a better solution for those eurozone member countries that were opposed to Germany's economic policies would have been to invite Germany itself to leave the eurozone. As he put it, rather than

> having each of the crisis countries leave, one by one, or the countries of the euro-zone stick together, mired in an ill-fated near-stagnation, there is an alternative solution: Germany and perhaps some other northern European countries … could leave. This would be an easier way to bring Europe back to health. (Stiglitz, 2016: 292)

Stiglitz's proposal illustrated the serious underestimation of the contribution that same-currency-denominated securities can make to the mass and gravitational force of a currency area. A eurozone without Germany may have helped to reduce trade imbalances within the zone, and at the same time allow for fiscal expansion, but there was also a huge downside to such a scenario, which is that given the contribution of Germany's securities to the euro capital markets (a contribution that was significant as much in a qualitative sense as in a quantitative one – German government bonds were for some time the only triple-A rated eurozone government securities) its exclusion from these markets would have severely reduced the euro's backing mass and thus weight of gravitational force in the global financial domain. This was not a result that would have been welcomed by France or by Italy or by any other of Germany's partners for whom a major rationale behind the creation of a large euro area was to provide protective shelter against global financial pressures and thereby prevent their currencies from ending up like the Curiatii. In the end, it was because this latter consideration weighed so heavily with so many of the eurozone's member countries that, for all of the eurozone's serious flaws that were exposed by the severity of its crisis, the eurozone emerged from that crisis intact and without the loss of a single member.

Although the eurozone now comprises 20 national economies whose combined percentage shares of world trade and production exceed those of the US economy, its currency's international standing is still very much junior to that of the US dollar principally because the eurozone's bond and equity markets continue to remain much smaller than those of the United States. There are strong reasons why the eurozone should expand its securities markets to a size and depth comparable with the US markets, thus giving the euro more international parity with the dollar, and we shall expand on these reasons in the final part of this book. For the present we must discount any suggestion that the eurozone project has turned out to be a failure on account of the fact that over the past 20 years and more of the euro's existence it has not managed to displace the dollar at the top of the international currency hierarchy.[5] On the contrary, for all the eurozone's design faults, the decision taken at the euro's launch to include all applicant countries has proved to be absolutely correct in that this currency was from the outset given enough backing quantities of financial securities as to make it a financial centre of gravity in its own right alongside the dollar. Rather, the failure has lain elsewhere. Looking to the example set by the eurozone, various groupings of emerging market economies (EMEs) across Asia, the Middle East and other regions seriously considered currency integration in the late 1990s and early 2000s, but none have been able to achieve this objective because of the many formidable impediments. This failure to form large regional currency blocs, coming at a time when international portfolio flow volumes were expanding at an exponential rate, was to have serious ramifications both for the EMEs themselves and for the world as a whole: for the former in that their currencies were to remain firmly trapped in the dollar's gravitational field and for latter in that it helped prepare the ground for the first great crisis of the 21st century. While the financial crisis of 2007–8 shared in common with the subsequent COVID-19 pandemic and Ukraine crises the fact that it served to consolidate the size asymmetry separating the US dollar markets from the EME financial markets, what distinguished the financial crisis was that this same size asymmetry was absolutely central to its causal origins.

PART II

Crises and the Consolidation of Dollar Dominance

THREE

The Financial Crisis of 2007–8

To understand the impact that the great financial crisis of 2007–8 had on the dollar's role as an international currency, it is first necessary to see whether that role had any bearing on the causal origins of the crisis. The crisis broke out in the United States, but if its causal origins in a structural as distinct from a purely geographical sense were also specific to that country, then the dollar's role as the world's leading currency could not have had any significant bearing on the events prior to the crisis while the events subsequent to the crisis could not have had any significant reverse bearing on the dollar's international role in the private sphere (the strengthening of that role in the official sphere as a result of the Federal Reserve's and other central banks' post-crisis actions are another matter). On the contrary, if the structural causes of the financial crisis were global in the sense that agents and institutions outside of the United States were as complicit in precipitating the crisis as were those inside the United States, then it follows that the dollar's international role had to have been a critical factor in the crisis and that events subsequent to the crisis had to have critically impacted that role. This latter position is the one that will be advanced here.

The financial products at the epicentre of the financial crisis of 2007–8 were a specific type of debt security, collateralized debt obligations (CDOs). The best way to understand these securities and their relation to the other, more conventional type of debt securities is to look at the 'floor', so to speak, where the source of the interest payments is to be found. Thus, where the bonds issued by governments and corporations are 'ground floor' securities in that the cash flows on them are serviced directly out of tax revenues or corporate profits, and where asset-backed securities (ABSs) issued by banks are 'first floor' securities in that the cash flows on them are serviced by the interest payments on loans (including mortgage loans), CDOs are essentially 'second floor' securities, structured financial products created by pooling non-conforming mortgage-backed securities (for example, securities backed by subprime loans) together with conforming mortgage-backed securities as collateral for CDOs. Although it was well known that non-conforming loans taken on their own could in no way serve as safe collateral, it was thought that this problem could be circumvented by first mixing the latter securities together with conforming loan-backed securities as collateral and then by using various techniques to enhance the creditworthiness of the structured securities. As it turned out, the same techniques that were intended to make CDOs safe by spreading risk also made them so complex as to make it difficult for them to be priced to any market standard. Thus, when the delinquency rate among US subprime borrowers began to rise sharply in the wake of the successive increases in the federal funds rate from mid-2004, not only did these sophisticated techniques not prevent a resulting fall in the prices of CDOs, they also helped to accelerate the rate of that fall by virtue of having helped to make these products too opaque and hence too difficult to value accurately. It was the panic caused by the unexpectedly rapid collapse of the CDO market that led to the breakdown in trust between the large commercial banks, a breakdown that proved to be catastrophic in that it was the catalyst setting in motion a liquidity-solvency crisis spiral that eventually culminated in the paralysis of the whole financial system.

In addition to the complexity and opacity of CDOs, a further major reason why the sudden collapse of the CDO market in the summer of 2007 triggered the financial crisis concerned the size that it had reached by that point in time. Although first established in the early 1980s, the CDO market remained very small up to about the end of 2003 when the outstanding volume of CDOs was then no more than about $250 billion. Had the market for CDOs continued to remain that small up to mid-2007, it is doubtful whether its sudden collapse at that point would have had much of an impact. The fact of the matter, however, is that it had by then grown 12-fold to about $3 trillion, in other words, to a size of sufficient proportions as to trigger the financial crisis (Lysandrou, 2012). Thus, a cardinal question concerning the crisis' origins is why had the market for the toxic CDOs grown so rapidly in so short a time span? In addressing this question, it is first necessary to distinguish between the factors that *enabled* rapid CDO growth and those that *motivated* this growth. There is wide agreement that among the major enabling factors in the CDO growth story was the pre-crisis failure of the financial regulatory authorities to extend any kind of capital adequacy and risk control rules to the various off-balance sheet financial entities and their securitization activities that collectively comprised what came to be known as the 'shadow banking' system. As the majority of these entities were owned or sponsored by the regulated commercial banks, the latter obviously stood to gain from engaging in 'regulatory arbitrage': for example, banks' mortgage loans to households would be packaged together, taken off their balance sheets and passed on to special purpose entities with interest payments set at rates slightly lower than those attaching to the original mortgage loans, while the special purpose entities would in turn use the loans as backing collateral for the creation of securities (the ABSs) that could be sold to an assortment of investors (including the structured investment vehicles that purchased ABSs to create the CDOs) with interest payments also set at rates slightly lower than those on the loans purchased from the parent or sponsoring banks, and so on in a cycle that could be repeatedly continued as the off-balance sheet vehicles were not obliged to keep to any specified capital-asset ratios.

Where there is fundamental disagreement is over the causal or motivating factor in the CDO growth story. The banks may have profited handsomely from engaging in regulatory arbitrage but what, exactly, drove them to continually expand the scale of this activity to the point where it reached crisis threatening proportions? The answer to this particular question that has until now been favoured by most economists is one that essentially puts the blame on psychological failings. The crux of the matter as viewed from this vantage point is that the privileged position occupied by banks in the financial system exposes them to certain temptations that in the end lead them to act irrationally and against their own self-interests. An example of how the causal origins of the financial crisis were interpreted within this psychological framework was a paper published in 2014 by Claudio Borio, chief economist at the Bank for International Settlements. According to Borio, the financial crisis exposed the 'Achilles heel' of the international financial system, which is its 'excess financial elasticity', a flaw that can be traced to 'powerful feedback mechanisms' that link together two limitations in financial agents' behaviour: one concerning their perceptions of value and risk, which 'are loosely anchored and highly procyclical' and the other concerning their incentives, which 'are inadequate to restrain risk-taking sufficiently during booms' (Borio, 2014: 3). Borio's basic explanation of how these powerful feedback mechanisms can eventually produce a crisis on the scale such as that witnessed in 2007–8 was as follows:

> As perceptions of risk decline, asset values surge and incentives to take on risk grow, so financing constraints become looser: external funding becomes cheaper and more ample (funding liquidity), and selling assets becomes easier and less expensive (market liquidity). Consequently, as the financial boom proceeds, it feeds on itself, sowing the seeds of its subsequent demise. (Borio, 2014: 3–4)

There is no doubt that, alongside lax financial regulation and regulatory arbitrage, bank overconfidence and a consequent undervaluation and mispricing of risk were important contributory factors in the financial crisis. What is in doubt is whether these latter factors were indeed the causal factors. What gives serious grounds for this doubt is the problem of *time indeterminacy*. As already noted, the US CDO market remained small up to 2003 after which point it then expanded 12-fold from $0.25 trillion to $3 trillion by mid-2007. The same was true of the US ABS market. These securities had existed since the early 1980s, but well over one half of the $9 trillion worth of US ABSs outstanding in 2007 had been created in the previous three years (Bank of England, 2007a). Now why was it that it was this particular three-year span between 2004 and 2007 that witnessed an explosive growth of both the ABS and CDO markets and not any earlier three-year span, one, say, in the late 1980s or early 1990s? The banking sector had in those earlier periods all the same opportunities and incentives and all the same financial engineering techniques to create ABSs and CDOs on a substantive scale, so why it did it wait until about 2004 before doing so? A plausible answer to this question lay in the very sudden acceleration in investor demand for US bonds as safe assets that occurred around the early 2000s and that emanated from three principal sources:

1. foreign central banks, and most notably those of China and other Asian countries, that required US treasury and agency bonds for exchange rate management purposes;
2. foreign institutional asset managers that, finding that there were not enough alternative currency-denominated securities to meet their portfolio needs, increasingly turned to the dollar markets to meet these needs;
3. US private investors that included US high net worth individuals along with US institutional investors (Goda and Lysandrou, 2014).

Given that there were economic limits to the rates at which the US government and its agencies and US corporations could increase their supplies of bonds, it was only logical that the US banking sector would step in and increase their rate of production of private label mortgage-backed securities (MBSs) and CDOs to help accommodate the global rise in investor safe asset demand. Of course, the US banks and their off-balance sheet vehicles stood to gain handsomely from this increase in their mortgage-backed securitization activities, but the timing of this increase strongly indicates that its primary cause lay with external investor asset demand pressures rather than with any internal profit-seeking motives. As the Massachusetts Institute of Technology-based economist Riccardo Caballero summed up these developments:

> The entire world, including foreign central banks and investors, but also many U.S. financial institutions, had an insatiable demand for safe debt instruments which put enormous pressure on the U.S. financial system and its incentives. ... This is not to say that the often emphasised regulatory and corporate governance weaknesses, misguided homeownership policies, and unscrupulous lenders, played no role in creating the conditions for the surge in real estate prices and its eventual crash. However, it is to say that these were mainly important in determining the minimum resistance path for the safe-assets imbalance to release its energy, rather than being the structural sources of the dramatic recent macroeconomic boom-bust cycle. (Caballero, 2010: 4)

Despite the close time fit between the foreign and domestic flows into the US government and corporate bond markets and the acceleration in MBS and CDO production, this was never accepted as sufficient proof of the safe asset demand explanation of the financial crisis by its critics. Claudio Borio, for example, found that the evidence for this explanation 'is not convincing' because

> strong demand for safe assets in the run-up to the Great Financial Crisis should have led to a widening, not a narrowing, of the spread between safe and risky assets. Associating this demand for safe assets with a search for yield is misleading, since higher demand for safety points to higher, not lower, risk aversion or risk perceptions. (Borio, 2014: 15)

An immediate problem with this argument is its implicit assumption that in the years prior to the crisis the world's investors were faced with a wide choice of different currency-denominated bonds in which to store their funds and were thus able to demand higher risk premiums on the riskier dollar bonds that they bought. The reality was that they had no such choice because no other currency region was able to generate bond supplies on scales anything like that of the United States. At a deeper theoretical level, Borio's critique of the search for yield explanation of the financial crisis is symptomatic of the theoretical subsumption of all investors under the representative household investor category. From this standpoint, it follows that any gap that opens up between the aggregate supply of securities, on the one hand, and the aggregate demand for them, on the other, can always be closed through the *price adjustment mechanism*: if borrowers issue less securities than are demanded, then the prices of these securities will go up and their yields go down, thus encouraging borrowers to issue more securities, while, conversely, if borrowers issue more securities than are demanded, then the prices of these securities must fall and their yields rise so as to generate the extra investor demand for them. Once this line of thinking is applied to the pre-crisis developments in the US debt securities markets, it must then follow that there cannot have been any excess demand pressures spilling over from one market to the next (from the ground floor government and corporate bond markets, to the first-floor ABS market, to the second-floor CDO market) simply because the equilibrating role of price adjustments would have eliminated any such pressures.

On the contrary, the fact that the banks were indeed responding to investor demand pressure when creating the toxic securities becomes clear when institutional investors such as pension funds in the private sector and central banks in the official sector are separated out as a fundamentally distinct group because what then becomes clear is that in the case of this group – for whom the holding of securities for value storage purposes is always a functionally driven necessity – any disequilibrium between supply and demand in the securities markets can only be resolved through a *quantity adjustment mechanism* and not through a price adjustment one. Thus, when the steep rise in both foreign and domestic institutional investors demand for US treasury bonds and for US federal-backed mortgage bonds ('agency bonds') from the early 2000s onwards led to a corresponding rise in their prices and, conversely, a corresponding fall in their yields, these latter movements did nothing to dampen the aggregate institutional demand for these bonds. Rather, this demand continued to rise and, as we say, it was to help absorb much of this demand pressure that the US banking sector stepped up its rate of production of private label MBSs and CDOs from about early 2005 onwards. It of course stands to reason that had the US private banking sector followed the example of the US government-backed agencies in only extending mortgage loans to creditworthy households there would have been no financial crisis of the form that broke out in the summer of 2007. The reality, however, was that there were economic limits to the numbers of such households that could be brought into the mortgage loan market and when those limits began to be reached by early 2005, the only feasible way of making up the shortfall in the mortgage loan material needed for securitization purposes was to bring in increasing numbers of borrowers who met few if any of the standard lending criteria into the mortgage loan market (Bank of England, 2007b).

A further reason why the regulatory arbitrage explanation of the financial crisis continues to be favoured by mainstream economists and official authorities relates to the involvement of the European banking sector in the US mortgage market in the pre-crisis period. Where the US banks operated the off-balance sheet entities that created the majority of the long-term mortgage-backed debt securities (the MBSs and CDOs), the European banks were the major operators of the off-balance sheet 'conduits' that supplied the short-term mortgage-backed securities, asset-backed commercial paper (ABCP), where the backing collateral used to create these securities ranged from ordinary mortgage loans to MBSs and CDOs. Now, as long as the interest rate paid to investors in ABCP remained lower than the rates received on the long-term backing assets, the conduits could generate profits. But when the panic that gripped the US financial sector in the summer of 2007 instantly spread to the ABCP market, causing the rate on this paper to rise precipitously, the ABCP conduits became insolvent, with the consequence that the parent banks came under huge financial pressure as they had typically given 100 per cent guarantees to their conduits without holding anything like the equivalent amount of capital backing. In the end, it was the European banks' double-sided involvement in the MBS, CDO and ABCP markets, selling ABCP to fund purchases of MBSs and CDOs that could be used as collateral for more ABCP issuance and so on in a continuum, that explains why these banks suffered immense damage on the outbreak of the financial crisis and hence why the destructive effects of the US financial crisis quickly engulfed Europe. This said, what is in question is whether the fact that the European banks had helped to expand the MBS, CDO and ABCP markets to dangerously high levels through their dollar credit intermediation activity meant that this activity and its accompanying undervaluation of risk were among the root causes of the 2007–8 crisis. This was the conclusion drawn by the Bank for International Settlements-based economist Robert McCauley in a paper published in 2018 where he compared the pre-crisis financial flows into the United States emanating from Asia with those emanating from Europe. Proceeding on the assumption that there was no connection whatsoever between the 'transpacific' and the 'transatlantic' inflows, he argued that the latter gave 'better satisfaction' as an explanation of the financial crisis because these inflows had been principally directed to the riskier, private label mortgage-backed products that were at the epicentre of the crisis while the inflows from Asia had been principally directed to the safer government and government-backed debt securities. As McCauley observed in his critique of those who had instead given explanatory primacy in the financial crisis to the Asian inflows:

> Focusing on the official inflow, Caballero (2010) saw it as chasing safe assets that Wall Street had a comparative advantage in producing. In fact, official reserve managers steered clear of risky private MBS, however rated. … Instead they hugged the shore of US Treasury bonds and US government-supported agency bonds. Those developing this thesis overlooked European banks' provision of safe assets to US money market funds. These banks invested the proceeds in pseudo-safe MBS, many rated AAA, in a so-called 'credit arbitrage' strategy which proved far riskier than expected. Official reserve managers demanded dollar safe assets; European banks supplied them. (McCauley, 2018: 40)

As we say, McCauley would have been entirely correct in favouring the credit arbitrage explanation of the crisis had there been no connection between the pre-crisis transatlantic flows into the US financial markets and the transpacific inflows. The truth of the matter is that there was a close connection, as becomes clear when considering the following list of facts that were salient to the European banks' pre-crisis involvement in the US ABCP market:

1. the European ABCP supply rate remained flat in the early 2000s up to the end of 2004, and only after that point did it then begin to rise rapidly through to mid-2007;
2. this rise in the ABCP supply rate was in direct response to the sudden steep rise in ABCP demand from the US institutional money market mutual funds that occurred towards the end of 2004;
3. the rise in ABCP demand was motivated by the rise in the federal funds rate to which the ABCP rate was closely tied up to the outbreak of the financial crisis;
4. the principal reason why the Federal Reserve raised the federal funds rate by a quarter percent in 17 consecutive months starting in June 2004 (so that from 1 per cent at that point it had reached 5.25 per cent by July 2006) was to contain the inflationary pressures that were building up in the US domestic economy;
5. the principal source of those inflationary pressures was not energy price rises as was initially thought, but the high rate of house price inflation that had facilitated a high rate of equity extraction that had in turn fuelled a consumer spending boom;
6. the principal source of the house price boom from 2004 onwards was the sudden acceleration in the rate of mortgage loan issuance;
7. this sudden acceleration was precipitated by the need to obtain the extra raw material needed to create the extra quantities of assets demanded by foreign investors for use as stores of value.

In sum, the pre-crisis transpacific financial flows into the United States, on the one side, and the pre-crisis transatlantic financial inflows, on the other, represented not two different storylines so much as two sides of the same investor asset demand storyline.[1]

We can now return to the subject of the dollar. As noted at the outset of this chapter, how one construes the causal origins of the financial crisis determines how one construes the relation between that crisis and the dollar's international role. Consider in this regard the build-up of events prior to the crisis. If one takes a bank overconfidence and risk undervaluation line of explanation of these events, it must follow that the dollar's international role cannot have been of any great relevance to the causal origins of the crisis given that that explanation places those origins firmly inside the United States. Foreign investors certainly needed dollars to access the US securities markets, but if these investors are seen to have merely played a secondary role as buyers of the products that the US banks sold to profit from regulatory arbitrage, then so also must the dollar's international role have only been of secondary importance. By contrast, put the investor bond demand explanation of the financial crisis and it must then follow that its structural origins were global in that agents and institutions outside of the United States were as complicit in causing the crisis as were those inside the United States. From this standpoint it must then also follow that the dollar's role as an international currency must have been of central importance inasmuch as that role was both instrumental to foreign central banks' acquisitions of US treasury and agency bonds for reserve management purposes and to foreign private investors' acquisitions of private label MBSs and CDOs for value storage purposes. Now consider the post-financial crisis situation. Put the overconfidence and risk undervaluation explanation of the crisis and it then follows that its after-effects could not have had any direct bearing on the dollar's international role in the private sphere. Rather, any bearing would have had to have been indirect in the negative sense that foreign investors, already concerned about the United States' deteriorating macroeconomic fundamentals, would have been further concerned about the weaknesses in the US financial system and would have consequently withdrawn substantial amounts of funds from the United States, thus weakening the dollar. Indeed, in the years immediately following the crisis there were many observers who predicted a foreign investor flight from the dollar and were subsequently bewildered when not only did this flight not happen, but the opposite happened as foreign investors actually increased their dollar investments. By contrast, this latter development is entirely in keeping with the investor bond demand explanation of the financial crisis, for if the dollar's international strength, based as it was on the size and depth of US securities markets, thereby helped to cause the crisis, the compliment was bound to be returned after the crisis because in causing widespread disruption and uncertainty in the capitalist world economy, and thus a corresponding increase in investor flight to the safety of US bonds, the crisis was bound to further strengthen the dollar's international position.

Just over a decade after the great financial crisis of 2007–8, the world economy was again hit by two successive major crises, one generated by the COVID-19 pandemic in 2020 and the other by Russia's invasion of the Ukraine in early 2022. The question that arises out of the juxtaposition of these three crises is whether there is any connecting link between them that involves in any way the dollar's international role. The answer has to be negative if one follows the majority explanation of the financial crisis of 2007–8, because that explanation sets the financial crisis in a business cycle framework and what this means is that any connecting link to other crises runs not forward to the present but backward to the past and to previous financial crises. Indeed, one of the reasons why the bank overconfidence explanation of the financial crisis has been favoured by most economists is that, absent the novelty of some of the products and practices that were central to the crisis, there was nothing fundamentally new about it in that the history of capitalism is replete with banking crises that have been caused by overconfidence and the undervaluation of risk on the part of the banks. It is in this context that Hyman Minsky's 'financial instability hypothesis', long ignored by the mainstream, suddenly attracted its attention on the outbreak of the financial crisis because that hypothesis seems to accurately capture bank behaviour over the course of the business cycle.[2] It is testimony of how 'Minsky became mainstream' following the financial crisis that in a speech marking its tenth anniversary in 2018 given by Mark Carney, the then governor of the Bank of England, Minsky's theory was repeatedly invoked to back up his point that the main lesson of the crisis was to dispel certain 'lies of finance', the first of which 'is the four most expensive words in the English language: "This Time is Different"' (Carney, 2018: 2). Following in the spirit of Minsky, Carney argued that just as in the case of all previous financial crises it was a sustained pre-crisis period of macroeconomic stability and rising asset prices that caused complacency on the part of the banks, so was this also true in the case of the great financial crisis in that the years of the 'Great Moderation' – a period marked by a highly unusual combination of strong growth, low unemployment and low inflation – also led to general complacency. What was particularly problematic in this latter case, and what gave added urgency to the lessons to be learnt, was that the complacency generated by the Great Moderation infected not just the private banking sector but also the regulatory authorities. As Carney put it: 'A deep-seated faith in markets lay beneath the new thinking of the Great Moderation. Captured by the myth that finance can regulate and correct itself spontaneously, authorities retreated from their regulatory and supervisory responsibilities' (Carney, 2018: 3). Driven by the conviction that this retreat from their regulatory and supervisory responsibilities was a major cause of the financial crisis, the financial authorities in the United States and in Europe moved with such speed after the crisis in bringing the shadow banking system under the regulatory umbrella that the result was a sharp contraction of the markets for CDOs, MBSs and other types of structured financial products. Seeing how successful their new tight regulation had been in preventing any repeat expansion of the toxic securities markets that were at the epicentre of the financial crisis, the financial authorities then confidently declared that there cannot be a repeat of the financial crisis of 2007–8. Time will tell whether this confidence is misplaced, but thus far there has been no similar financial crisis given that the COVID-19 pandemic and Ukraine crises in no way fit into this mould.

Now let us turn to the investor bond demand explanation of the financial crisis. The first thing to note is that from this vantage point the crisis had no historical precedent, that, indeed, *this time was different.* There have been earlier periods when bond demand outran bond supply, but what was fundamentally different about the pre-2007 period was the growing imbalance between the *globally* dispersed nature of bond demand and the *locally* concentrated nature of bond supply. Recall that the closing years of the 20th century marked both the globalization of capitalism (in that virtually all independent nation states now operate to the same market exchange principle) and the financialization of capitalism (in that this marked the first time that the world's financial securities markets, and particularly the world's government and corporate bond markets, begin to systematically outgrow the world's product markets). Although contemporaneous, the outcomes of these two developments were far from compatible in that while globalization led through one route or another to a growth in investor demand for bonds for value storage purposes that was widely dispersed across different countries and regions, the volume supply of those bonds remained heavily concentrated in just one country: the United States. Thus, when the excess bond demand pressures outside of the United States steadily built up, it was inevitable that those pressures would eventually find vent inside the United States and end up precipitating the financial crisis. Now the new regulatory measures introduced after the crisis may have radically reduced the markets for structured debt securities as we have noted, but they did nothing to reduce the size asymmetry separating the US bond markets from those of other regions. Quite the contrary, in fact, because that size asymmetry continued to grow by orders of magnitude.

If we take the case of all the world's emerging market economies (EMEs) bar China, we find that in 2010 their combined share of the $82.2 trillion worth of bonds then outstanding was a mere $1.4 trillion, a figure not only very small as compared with the United States' total contribution of $30.2 trillion but also very small as compared merely with the US government's contribution of $8.8 trillion. Moving forward to 2019, we find that where by then the United States' total bond volumes had risen to $41.2 trillion, with the contribution made by treasuries nearly doubling to $16.7 trillion, the corresponding increase for the world's EMEs was just $0.7 trillion, from $1.4 trillion in 2010 to $2.1 trillion in 2019. The major explanation for these very differing developments was of course the difference in government borrowing costs. A key factor enabling the US government to substantially raise its borrowing volumes after the financial crisis was the trend decline in its borrowing costs; the yield on ten-year treasuries, for example, fell from 3.2 per cent in 2010 to 2.1 per cent in 2019 (SIFMA, 2023). In stark contrast, EME government borrowing costs continued to remain substantially higher than those faced by the US government, the yield premiums on EME government bonds over US treasuries ranging from 4–5 per cent on the upper rated AA and BBB bonds to 15 per cent on the lower rated CCC bonds (OECD, 2021). A central factor behind this divergence in government borrowing costs were the differential roles played by foreign investors, an enabling role in the case of the US government as the decline in its borrowing costs was greatly facilitated by the continuing increase in foreign purchases of treasuries (where in 2006, the year before the financial crisis, foreign investors held $2.1 trillion worth of treasuries, by 2010 that figure had more than doubled to $4.5 trillion and by 2019 it had more than trebled to $6.7 trillion) and a constraining role in the case of EME governments. Thus, where the severe disruption to the world economy and the prolonged ensuing uncertainty caused by the financial crisis had led to a fall in US borrowing costs as the world's institutional investors here traded yield off against safety, that same disruption and ensuing uncertainty had precisely the opposite effect on EME governments' borrowing costs as institutional investors demanded higher risk premiums in line with the increase in uncertainty.

With this discussion in mind, it is now possible to see a connection running from the financial crisis of 2007–8 through to the later COVID-19 pandemic and Ukraine crises that centrally involves the dollar's international dominance. The heart of the matter is that if this dominance principally rests on the fact that US securities markets are large relative to those of other countries, this size asymmetry is no longer one that is determined solely by factors that are internal to the United States and to other countries. In the era before the globalization and financialization of capitalism, the United States had comparatively large equity and bond markets because it could combine together such determining factors as a large production base, strong legal and governance infrastructure, and certain propitious cultural traditions in a way that no other country could. Although restrictions on international financial flows began to be comprehensively lifted in the 1970s and 1980s, these flows were still not large and powerful enough to act as an additional determinant of financial market size asymmetries. The situation subsequently changed radically as international financial flows were considerably swelled both by the influx of the Asian and ex-communist countries into the capitalist orbit and by the steep volume growth of the world's securities markets relative to the world's product markets. Now while the increase in these flows in the early to mid-1990s may have then been more associated with speculatively driven surges, by the late 1990s and early 2000s the flow increase had come to be more closely associated with the increasing internationalization of institutionally managed asset portfolios. It is principally because heavy international portfolio flows have become regularized in tandem with the structural changes in the global asset management industry that they have become an important external determinant of the respective sizes of countries' securities markets with the result that these sizes no longer remain independent of each other as they had been when determined by internal factors alone. Rather, and as explained in an earlier chapter, they are now interdependent as the dollar markets become comparatively larger over time because of the advantages to foreign investors offered by their core position in the global financial system, while, conversely, other currency-denominated securities markets, and particularly those based in the EMEs, become comparatively smaller over time because of the higher yields demanded by foreign investors as compensation for their smallness. It is here that global crises enter the picture because if international portfolio flows now constitute one of the mechanisms through which the majority of the world's securities markets are kept subordinate to the dollar markets, global crises are now part of the mainsprings of that mechanism. The financial crisis of 2007–8 was the first crisis of its kind because this was the first time that there arose too big an imbalance between the global nature of safe asset demand and the local nature of safe asset supply, but what was also new about the financial crisis is that it was the first to help amplify the size of the US financial markets relative to other markets and hence amplify the strength of the dollar relative to other currencies by causing severe economic disruption and investor flight to safety. In this respect it set a precedent that was to be followed by subsequent global crises.

FOUR

The COVID-19 and Ukraine Crises

The COVID-19 pandemic that broke out in China at the end of 2019 placed government finances under strains even heavier than those generated by the financial crisis of 2007–8. The reasons for this included the fact that the economic costs of the COVID-19 pandemic came on top of the healthcare costs that had to be borne by governments, the fact that it was not just one group of firms in one economic sector that had to be protected from bankruptcy by government bailout loans but a whole range of firms drawn from across the entire domestic economy, and the fact that on this occasion governments had to fund not only business bailouts but also the wages of employees that had been temporarily laid off while also bearing the financial costs of the soaring levels of unemployment. In the case of the emerging market economy (EME) governments, there were the added factors that, on top of the huge health problems and huge disruption to their domestic production and employment levels caused by the pandemic, they also faced falls in their export earnings caused by the contraction of their overseas markets, falls in the price of oil and in other commodity prices, falls in remittances from abroad and last, but not least, falls in incomes from a range of tourism and other travel-related services. The paradox is that while EME governments had greater cause than their advanced market economy (AME) counterparts to rely on bond issuance to help manage the costs incurred by the COVID-19 pandemic, they were far less able to do so because the bond issuance terms that they faced were as onerous as they were favourable for their AME counterparts.

In 2020 governments across the Organisation for Economic Co-operation and Development (OECD) area issued around $18 trillion worth of marketable debt securities, a gross figure that was double the $9 trillion issued in 2008 following the outbreak of the financial crisis, and significantly higher than the average annual rate of issuance that plateaued at around $10.5 trillion in the decade 2009–19 (OECD, 2020a; 2021). Subtracting the amounts needed for maturing bond redemptions, the net issuance of OECD sovereign bonds in 2020 was around $5 trillion, a sum two and a half times the average $2 trillion figure for the period 2009–19. Although the rate of OECD sovereign bond issuance abated somewhat in 2021, the figures of $15 trillion and $3 trillion for gross and net issuance respectively were still appreciably higher than the averages for the preceding decade. A key factor enabling OECD governments to raise such vast sums in so short a period were the exceptionally favourable yields that were paid out on their debt. In the wake of the financial crisis, the average yield on OECD ten-year sovereign bonds had trended down from around 5 per cent in 2008 to around 1.5 in 2019, but that average then fell again to around 1 per cent in 2020, where it remained all through 2021, with several governments (including those of Germany, Sweden and the Netherlands) even recording negative yields over this two-year period (OECD, 2022). While the quantitative easing policies of OECD countries' central banks, key to which were their substantial purchases of their governments' bonds, helped to keep down OECD sovereign borrowing costs, the major enabling factor in this regard were the heavy investment flows into sovereign bonds from pension funds and other institutional investors seeking safe harbour for their assets.

When we turn to the case of EME governments, the contrasts as regard both borrowing volumes and borrowing costs could not be starker. In 2020, EME government bond gross issuance came to about $3.4 trillion, a sum higher than the average $2.4 trillion figure for the decade 2009–19 but substantially less than the aggregate OECD figure of $18 trillion and even less than the $3.9 trillion worth of treasuries issued by the US government alone. A fact just as remarkable as that concerning the comparatively small increase in the amount of total EME government bond issuance in 2020 is that not all regional EME governments were able to contribute to this increase. While all of the AME governments were able to issue more bonds that year relative to the amounts issued in 2019, the same was not true of EME governments in that a substantial number of them, notably those based in Latin America, the Middle East and North Africa, and Sub-Saharan Africa, actually issued less bonds in 2020 compared to the previous year's issuance (OECD, 2021). The constraining factors involved in all of this were, of course, the exceptionally high yields that had to be paid out to investors. EME sovereign bonds divide into the investment grade (AA to BBB) and non-investment grade (BB down to CCC and lower) categories, both of which continued to carry substantial yield premiums over the benchmark US treasury rate over the decade 2009–19 (around 4 per cent for AA and BBB, around 5 per cent for BB, and an average of around 15 per cent for CCC). When the sheer scale of the COVID-19 pandemic's destructive global economic impact became fully evident by March 2020, the consequent effect on EME sovereign bond yields from that month through to July was the exact opposite of that on AME sovereign bond yields, for over that four-month period yields on AA and BBB rated EME sovereign bonds averaged around 7 per cent, while the yields on BB rated bonds averaged around 11 per cent and those on CCC rated bonds averaged a staggering 45 per cent. It is testimony to how wide was the gap between AME and EME government bond yields all through 2020 that the FTSE Ten Year Government Bond World Index rose by 1 per cent from 2 per cent to 3 per cent by the end of that year even while the aggregate amount of EME government bonds issued over this period was a small fraction of the world total amount of government bond issuance (OECD, 2021).

One of the major reasons why the bond issuance costs faced by EME governments at the outbreak of the COVID-19 pandemic were so different to those faced by AME governments is that the role played by large institutional investors in the EME countries is different to that played by them in the AME countries: where in the latter case, institutional investors help to lower government borrowing costs in times of economic disruption by switching funds away from higher risk corporate securities into the safety of government bonds, in the former case institutional investors on the contrary help to force up government borrowing costs in times of disruption by switching funds away from all EME securities, including EME government bonds, and into the safety of AME government bonds. We therefore find that the sudden upward spike in the risk premiums on all classes of EME government bonds that occurred in early March 2020 coincided with the withdrawal of over $30 billion worth of foreign portfolio funds from the EMEs (Hördahl and Shim, 2020). Over the following months in 2020 and into 2021, foreign portfolio investors steadily returned to the EMEs because, having stored the bulk of their funds in safe but low (or even negative) yielding AME government bonds, they needed to find extra yield somewhere and that somewhere included EME government debt. The AME government that most benefited from the investor flight to safety at the outset of the COVID-19 pandemic was the US government. While the outstanding amount of US treasury bonds rose from $16.67 trillion in 2019 to $20.93 trillion in 2020 and to $22.58 trillion in 2021, the yields on all tenors were kept low (those on the ten-year treasuries, for example, fell from to 2.14 per cent in 2019 to 0.88 per cent in 2020 while rising to 1.44 per cent in 2021 [OECD, 2021]), a principal contributory factor being the continually high proportion of these bonds held by foreign central banks and by foreign private institutional investors (thus, from $6.84 trillion in 2019, the total amount of US treasuries held by foreign investors rose to $7.07 trillion in 2020 and to $7.77 trillion in 2021 [SIFMA, 2022]).

Just when the world economy was recovering from the disruption caused by the COVID-19 pandemic it was dealt another major shock following Russia's invasion of the Ukraine in February 2022, the effects of which on this occasion were transmitted via the inflationary impact of the increase in oil and gas prices caused by Russia's cutbacks on its energy supplies to the West. To counter the inflationary pressures, central banks across the world immediately switched to a policy of monetary tightening with the result that baseline interest rates across the OECD area rose from an average of 0.8 per cent at the end of 2021 to an average of 5.3 per cent by the end of 2022. This switch in monetary policy after more than a decade of monetary easing inevitably impacted the yields and hence prices of financial securities. Thus, where equity prices had trended upwards on the back of quantitative easing so that from a nominal world total of $57 trillion in 2009, the nominal value of global equity stocks had reached $126 trillion in 2021, there was such a stark decline in equity prices following the switch to monetary tightening that that nominal world total had fallen back to $96 trillion in 2022. In the case of bonds, the fall in their prices and consequent rise in their yields was countered by a sustained rate of bond issuance such that the nominal value of the outstanding global bond stocks at the end of 2022 was $126 trillion, a figure not far off that for the previous year. Nowhere were the contrasting effects of monetary tightening equity and bond volumes more manifest than in the United States, for where the total nominal value of US equity stocks had fallen by almost a half from $80.09 trillion at the end of 2021to $41 trillion at the end of 2022, the corresponding figures for US bonds remained roughly the same, $50.1 trillion at the end of 2022 as distinct from $52.7 trillion at the end of 2021 (SIFMA, 2022).

The Ukraine crisis' negative impact on the world's EMEs from February 2022 onwards was hardly less substantive than that wrought by the COVID-19 pandemic two years earlier although the route through which that impact was transmitted was different. While some EMEs that are net exporters of energy or food products were to some extent protected from the inflationary effects of the Ukraine conflict, these effects were particularly catastrophic for other energy- and food-import dependent EMEs because what compounded the rise in commodity import prices was the depreciation of their currencies relative to the dollar that had strengthened considerably on the back of increased foreign investment flows into the United States. As happened at the outbreak of the COVID-19 pandemic, the outbreak of the Ukraine crisis triggered an immediate withdrawal of substantial amounts of foreign portfolio funds from the EMEs, with the United States again being the main recipient of the funds. The difference this time is that when portfolio investment flows returned to the EMEs in the search for yield, the yields demanded by foreign investors were significantly higher than was the case following the COVID-19 pandemic because the benchmark risk-free rate set by that on US treasuries was now in the 3 per cent range as compared with the previous 0.5 per cent range. Thus, where EME governments whose bonds remained either in the investment grade category (AA, A and BBB) or in the upper non-investment grade category (BB) had to pay out risk-adjusted yields of around 7–8 per cent and 9–10 per cent respectively, EME governments whose bonds were in the lower non-investment grade categories faced such exorbitant risk premiums as to force many of them out of the financial markets altogether. That the EME (ex-China) share of the $126 trillion global bond volume outstanding at the end of 2022 was 6.1 per cent, a percentage share slightly higher than was registered in 2019, was due to the fact that the net decline in government bond issuance in some regions, most notably in Sub-Saharan Africa, the Middle East and North Africa, and Latin America, was again countered by the net increase in bond issuance in other regions, and most notably in Asia.

The shock to the world economy dealt by the Ukraine crisis may have had different monetary policy ramifications as compared with those that were consequent on the shocks dealt by the financial crisis and the COVID-19 pandemic generated crisis, but there was absolutely no difference as regards the ramifications for the dollar's position in the international currency hierarchy. As already observed, the dollar's share of the $7.5 trillion daily forex turnover volume in 2022, two years into the COVID-19 pandemic and almost one year into the Ukraine conflict, remained at 44 per cent, the same percentage figure recorded in the previous Bank for International Settlements triennial surveys. This consistency in the dollar's high share of forex turnover was matched, first, by a consistency in the United States' high percentage contribution both to global bond volumes (39 per cent of the $128 trillion bond volume outstanding at the end of 2021 and 38.5 per cent of the $126 trillion bond volume outstanding at the end of 2022) and to global equity volumes (43 per cent of the $128 trillion figure for the end of 2021 and 42 per cent of the $96 trillion figure for the end of 2022) and, second, by a consistency in the growth volume of foreign investment flows into the US securities markets. This sequence of facts is in line with our argument that global economic crises, whatever their causal origin, will reinforce rather than undermine dollar dominance because they will inevitably reinforce the size and depth of the dollar's backing mass of financial securities as foreign investors increase their holdings of these securities in the interests of safety. Conversely, the fact that the combined EME currency share of the 2022 daily forex turnover figure remained fixed at around 13 per cent as on previous occasions, combined with the fact that this percentage matched that for the EME aggregate average share of bond and equity volumes outstanding at the end of 2022, as was also the case on previous occasions, are in line with our argument that crises will inevitably reinforce the dollar's gravitational pull over the smaller EME currencies as the higher risk premiums on their EME investments demanded by foreign portfolio investors will inevitably constrain the expansion of the EME securities markets and thus their ability to give EME currencies enough backing mass as to enable them to resist the dollar's gravitational force.

This conclusion regarding the Ukraine crisis' impact on dollar dominance may seem premature given that it has been drawn so soon after the outbreak of the crisis. Indeed, there are many commentators who have argued that while the events set in motion by Russia's invasion of the Ukraine had no discernible negative effect on the dollar in the months immediately following that invasion, they must eventually have such an effect. The merits of this argument will be evaluated more closely in the next chapter, but here we first consider whether the aim of achieving de-dollarization was central to Russia's calculations when invading the Ukraine in early 2022. In addressing this question, we must distinguish between two senses in which de-dollarization can be defined: a weak sense in that this merely refers to a rise in the proportion of international transactions using the renminbi and other currencies as alternatives to the dollar, and a strong sense in that de-dollarization would eventually culminate in the substitution of a bipolar or even multipolar currency for the present dollar-centred unipolar system. Already under way before the Ukraine invasion, de-dollarization defined in the weak sense was certain to gather momentum after the invasion given that the United States and its allies were certain to impose heavier than usual sanctions on Russia and given that Russia and its allies were equally certain to mount a commensurate response to these sanctions. However, it is a big leap to the further proposition that the events set in train by the Ukraine crisis will ultimately lead to de-dollarization defined in the strong sense and yet Russia and some of its allies have been more than ready to make this leap in their thinking. In this they seem to have been inspired by the lesson of history. Just as the pound sterling lost its top position in the currency hierarchy not at the precise point that Britain lost its top position as an industrial power so much as when the United States took the conscious decision to face outwards and assume leadership of the capitalist world at the end of the Second World War, then so also must the dollar suffer the same fate at the point where other countries are ready to take advantage of the United States' long deteriorating economic fundamentals and make a concerted effort to bring about the dollar's dethronement.

That point appears to have been reached because there are now many countries that have sufficiently strong motivation to abandon the dollar given the rising frequency with which the United States has used the dollar as an economic and political weapon, and because there are now in place such organizational frameworks as can facilitate a coordinated abandonment of the dollar on the scale necessary to make that abandonment effective. Foremost among these frameworks is the BRICS association of nations. First established in 2009, and then expanded in 2010 to include South Africa alongside Brazil, Russia, India and China, this association has always had as one of its principal objectives the strong de-dollarization of the global financial system. As Russia's President, Dimitry Medvedev, stated when hosting the first BRICS Summit in Yekaterinburg in 2009 following the financial crisis, a key purpose of the summit was not only to explore how to 'overcome the crisis' but also to 'discuss the parameters for a new financial system' (Medvedev, 2009). Already constituting a fairly formidable force in the world economy, many of the BRICS governments believe that their de-dollarization initiatives can be achieved providing enough other countries across Latin America, Africa and Asian follow their lead, and what sustains this belief is the example that was set by the dollar's eventual dethronement of the pound. It is illustrative of this point that in a study published in early 2022 under the title *Can BRICS De-dollarize the Global Financial System?* the affirmative answer to this question given by its authors was prompted by the study's

> underlying assumption that the dominant currency status of the US dollar may not be permanent. The US dollar's displacement of the previous hegemonic currency, namely, the British pound sterling, attests to this notion. The importance of examining BRICS' challenge to the US dollar's dominance lies in the group's collective economic power. BRICS accounts for 24 percent of world GDP and over 16 percent of world trade. … Thus, BRICS' de-dollarization activities would not only impact inter-BRICS financial relations but also create a ripple effect globally. (Papa and Liu, 2022: 2)

That 'ripple effect globally' has certainly been amplified by the West's reaction to Russia's invasion of the Ukraine for, on the one side, that reaction has boosted the number of countries applying for membership of the BRICS association (which currently amounts to more than 40), and, on the other side, it has boosted the BRICS determination to expand the range of policy initiatives to help achieve de-dollarization (these include the establishment of rival, non-dollar based international settlement and clearing systems, the introduction of central bank digital currencies and the expansion of central bank swap arrangements).

It is the declared determination on the part of BRICS and their allies to do all that can be done to reduce their dependence on the dollar that explains why the stream of predictions of a coming end to dollar dominance before the Ukraine invasion turned into a flood in the months following that invasion. Consider, for example, a series of articles published in the *Financial Times* in early 2023. In January of that year, Zoltan Pozsar argued that we shall soon see a multipolar international currency system that matches a multipolar international economic system because 'if the G20 fractures into the camps of the G7 plus Australia, Brics+ and the non-aligned, it's impossible that these rifts will not affect the international monetary system' as the 'dollar-based monetary order is already being challenged in multiple ways' (Pozsar, 2023). In his article published a month later in February, Nouriel Roubini essentially agreed with Zoltan Pozsar's position but with the difference that 'in a world that will be increasingly divided into two geopolitical spheres of influence – namely those surrounding the US and China – it is likely that a bipolar, rather than a multipolar, currency regime will eventually replace the unipolar one' (Roubini, 2023). As to the timing of this eventuality, Roubini went so far as to predict that the United States' declining share of world production coupled with China and its allies' attempts to hasten de-dollarization through the introduction of new technologies including central bank digital currencies and alternatives to SWIFT will mean that 'the relative decline of the US dollar as the main reserve currency is likely to occur over the next decade'. Finally, in her article published in March 2023 under the heading 'Prepare for a multipolar currency system', Gillian Tett argued that, while there is no immediate threat to dollar dominance, the emergence of a multipolar currency system seemed to be 'a sensible medium-term bet' given the palpable shift in trade invoicing patterns as China and her allies increasingly use the renminbi and other local currencies as alternatives to the dollar for invoicing and settling trade and payments (Tett, 2023). Concerned, if not exactly alarmed, by the rising tide of predictions of a coming end to dollar dominance the *Financial Times* ran an editorial in April 2023 under the heading 'Threats to dollar dominance are overblown'. Following its opening terse statement that 'the dollar's demise is vastly exaggerated', the editorial pointed to the various factors that continue to sustain the dollar's dominance such as that America still maintains its 'status as the world's largest economy and geopolitical powerhouse' and that the dollar 'is the currency of choice for international trade, accounting for more than four-fifths of trade finance and half of trade invoice' (*Financial Times* Editorial Team, 2023). Nevertheless, forceful as was the editorial's rebuttal of the dollar pessimists, it did nothing to stem the flow of predictions of the dollar's coming dethronement. There can be no better illustration of this point than that Wolfgang Munchau, a regular contributor to the *Financial Times'* opinion column and therefore someone who would have been fully aware of the paper's editorial on the dollar, could still publish an article in the New Statesman just two weeks later, in early May 2023, under the heading 'Why China and her allies are well placed to topple the dollar' (Munchau, 2023).

The reality is that China and its allies will not topple the dollar any time soon or at any time in the foreseeable future because the paradigmatic shift in global capitalism brought on by its financialization now means that a currency's position at the top of the international currency hierarchy is primarily determined by the comparative size of the issuing country's capital markets rather than by the comparative size of its production base. If those in the East have yet to recognize this paradigm shift, it is largely because it has yet to be universally recognized in the West. There is in the West an acceptance that the dollar's international strength now rests less on the United States' production sector than on its financial sector but, as there is also here an acceptance that this latter sector cannot provide the dollar with anything like the same solid foundations as the US production sector had previously done, it is also widely accepted that the dollar is ultimately at the mercy of foreign investors, its strength dependent on their grace and goodwill. As was previously argued, what gives room to this position is the failure to hammer home the value storage capacity of the securities that are the stuff of the US financial markets. For further illustration of this failure, let us go back to the *Financial Times'* editorial of 19 April 2023. It explained that the reasons why threats to the dollar are overblown are that the 'the greenback's eminence is reinforced by its enormous liquidity, America's openness to trade and investment, and trust in its supporting institutions'. This list of some of the important aspects of the US financial system that attract foreign investors is absolutely correct, yet what is missing is any reference to the one aspect that is the most vital of all: the *quantum* aspect. Yes, foreign investors are attracted by the liquidity of the dollar markets because it allows them to transfer funds cheaply and efficiently across different securities according to circumstances; yes, they are attracted by the openness of the dollar markets because it allows them to move investments into and out of these markets at will; and, yes, they are attracted by the United States' supporting institutions because they guarantee their rights as outside investors. But the issue that is of central concern to foreign investors, and which gives context and meaning to the other issues of liquidity, openness and trust, is the US ability to supply them with an abundance of value containers in which they can safely park their funds. It is this cardinal fact that no other country or region in the world can come close to the United States in supplying securities on the scale needed by portfolio and other institutional investors that explains why it is not the United States that is at the mercy of its foreign investors but the exact reverse: it is foreign investors that are at the mercy of the United States. Whatever the actions of the United States and however unpalatable these may be to foreign investors, they will not withdraw funds from its financial markets on the scale necessary to hurt the dollar because there is simply nowhere else for them to go. This same point explains why the United State's rising trade deficits with Asia and other regions, far from putting it at a geo-economic or geo-political disadvantage, on the contrary puts the US government in a strong position to weaponize its import tariffs because it knows that most of the countries that are heavily on exports to the United States are also heavily dollar asset dependent. In sum, no one should be under any illusion that dollar dominance will end soon as the United States' opponents 'chip away' at the current dollar-centred international currency transaction network. The reality is that no amount of chipping away at this network will have any palpable impact on dollar dominance as long as there continues to be a substantial size gap separating the US financial markets from all other markets, and that size gap will not be closed by BRICS, or by China taken separately, as we shall now see.

FIVE

Why BRICS or China Alone Will Not Challenge the Dollar

A major reason why the authors of the recent study *Can BRICS De-dollarize the Global Financial System?* gave an affirmative answer to the study's titular question was that 'the BRICS' de-dollarization activities would not only impact inter-BRICS financial relations but also create a ripple effect globally' (Papa and Liu, 2022: 2). To set this 'ripple effect' in context, consider two crucial facts regarding daily forex turnover volume that is now in the region of $7.5 trillion. The first concerns the percentage share of this volume that is accounted for by cross-emerging market economy (EME) currency transactions. Recall that as compared against the dollar's 44 per cent share of daily forex turnover, the combined share of all the EME currencies (which includes the currencies of all of the BRICS [Brazil, Russia, India, China and South Africa] group of countries and of all her allies) is about 13 per cent. However, if we subtract from this figure the EME currency transactions that involve either the dollar or the euro or even some other advanced market economy currency as the counterparty currency, it then turns out that the share of cross-EME currency transactions comes to no more than about 3 per cent. The second crucial fact regarding forex turnover that closely ties in with the first concerns the percentage share of real economy related currency transactions, that is to say, transactions relating either to trade in material goods and services or to foreign direct investments. The current estimate is that these transactions amount to about 8 per cent of the daily forex turnover volume. Now if we strip out from this percentage the real sector transactions that involve the United States or other advanced market economies as the counterparty to these transactions, it then again turns out that the cross-EME transactions relating to trade or to foreign direct investments come to no more than about 3 per cent. The upshot of all this is that no matter how much the BRICS group of countries and its allies succeed in increasing the use of various alternative currencies to the dollar for trade and investment purposes, the fact that the baseline starting point of this increase is so incredibly small means that it will have no discernible effect on the primacy of the dollar.

Further confirmation that finance-related transactions overwhelmingly dominate daily foreign exchange turnover volume is provided by its compositional breakdown according to institution. Banks are obviously the lead institutions in the foreign exchange markets given their intermediary role, with the main reporting banks accounting for about 50 per cent of the current $7.5 trillion daily turnover figure and the non-reporting banks accounting for an additional 22 per cent. Of the non-bank sector's contribution to forex turnover volume, we find that this too is dominated by financial institutions in that where institutional investors and hedge funds respectively account for 11 per cent and 8 per cent of this volume, non-financial corporations account for a mere 6 per cent. Now if the primacy of the dollar over all other currencies in the foreign exchange market links in with the primacy of finance-related transactions over production-related transactions and with the primacy of banks and other financial institutions over non-financial institutions, all of these respective primacies in their turn link in with the primacy of the dollar-denominated stocks of financial securities over all other currency-denominated stocks. To track the linkages, let us start with the world's institutional investors such as pension funds and insurance companies. Attracted to the US bond and equity markets because of the various advantages offered by their depth and liquidity, foreign institutional investors then add to their depth and liquidity and, in so doing, to the depth and liquidity of the dollar market itself. This latter addition then further reinforces a multiplier effect insofar as the use of dollars as means of accessing the US capital markets then reinforces the use of dollars in a number of other contexts. Thus, when portfolio funds are moved across countries with small securities markets, these movements typically take place via the dollar as the intermediary currency rather than via a direct pairwise exchange of the local currencies in question. If we take the case of the hedge funds that now account for much of the short-term speculative activity in the forex market (their use of computerized high frequency trading being particularly important in this context) we find that when trading the same pair of currencies many times over to extract profit from any small exchange rate movements, it is invariably the dollar that stands on one side of these pairwise currency transactions due to the depth and liquidity of the dollar market.

If we return to the top participants in the foreign exchange market, the reporting banks, we find not only that these institutions account for nearly one half of the daily forex turnover volume of $7.5 trillion but also that about a half of their forex activity is in foreign exchange (FX) swaps, instruments that account for about a half of all forex turnover and out of which about a half again have the dollar as one of the counterparty currencies. Once more, it is the size of the US capital markets that is at the root of these close correlations. All the major banks of the advanced market economies hold substantial amounts of foreign currency assets for various reasons that include those to do with self-interest business expansion as also those to do with serving the foreign currency needs of their institutional clients. But, this said, what is noteworthy is that the US banks hold far less foreign currency assets as compared, say, with the dollar assets held by their peers in the eurozone or in the UK, an asymmetry that clearly reflects the size asymmetry separating the dollar capital markets from those of the euro and sterling markets. Dollar-dominated FX swaps enter the picture here in that there are basically two ways in which non-US banks can fund their dollar assets, one through borrowing from deposits or from the money markets and the other through FX swaps. As few non-US banks have substantial operations inside the United States, thus limiting their ability to borrow from dollar deposits, the remaining main ways of funding their dollar assets is through accessing the dollar money markets (for example, through the issuance of commercial paper) or through FX swaps, but as the risk on dollar debt issuance tends to be higher than that on FX swaps (a fact that became particularly pronounced with the outbreak of the 2007 subprime crisis when there was a sharp rise in short term borrowing costs) the latter have continued to gain in popularity as dollar funding instruments.

We turn now to the dollar's position as a reserve currency, where it currently accounts for 58 per cent of all central bank held reserves as compared with the euro's 22 per cent and the 20 per cent accounted for by an assortment of other currencies. While the dollar's position in the official sphere is greater than that in the private sphere, where it accounts for 44 per cent of the $7.5 trillion daily forex turnover, it should be noted that where the dollar has essentially maintained this same percentage share in the private sphere over the past two decades, the same is not true as regards its share of officially held reserves that has declined from about 70 per cent in 2000 to the current 58 per cent. Given that this decline was already being taken as firm evidence of the erosion of dollar dominance before Russia's invasion of the Ukraine, it was inevitable that the invasion, by triggering a series of countermeasures against the US-led imposition of sanctions on Russia, would be seen to act as a catalyst giving added momentum to that erosion. This was the position taken by Barry Eichengreen, for example, in an article published in the *Financial Times* in March 2022, under the heading 'Ukraine war accelerates the stealth erosion of dollar dominance'. Observing that the share of dollars in globally identified foreign exchange reserves had been 'trending down' so that they now account for under 60 per cent of these reserves as opposed to the 70 per cent figure of 20 years ago, Eichengreen explained that the principal cause of this downward trend was central banks' diversification away from dollars towards the currencies of smaller economies, a diversification facilitated on the one hand by the liquidity of these markets and hence the low costs of transacting in them (all made possible by the advent of electronic trading platforms and other financial innovations) and motivated on the other hand by the attraction of the higher yields offered by the smaller currencies in contrast to those offered by the large currencies. While the reasons behind the diversification of their reserves away from the dollar by the central banks of Russia and of certain of her allies may be more political than financial in nature, this development nevertheless appears to have given good cause for drawing the conclusion, as does Eichengreen, that 'we are seeing movement towards a more multipolar international monetary system' (Eichengreen, 2022).

The immediate objection to this conclusion concerns the interpretation placed on the decline of the dollar's share of allocated reserves from 70 per cent in 2000 to under 60 per cent today. To say that there was a 'trend' decline in the dollar's share over this 20-year period is misleading because it gives the impression of a continuous, year-on-year decline. Rather, while there was an initial downward adjustment of the dollar's share to about 60 per cent that occurred after 2002 following the introduction of the euro in hard currency form, from that time to 2020 this percentage share then remained fairly stable, as did the euro's share of around 20 per cent, and as did the remaining 20 per cent collective share of several other smaller currencies. Now it is true that over the past three years the dollar's share of reserves has registered a further small decline so that it now stands at 58 per cent and it may well be that it will also register further small declines as central banks continue to diversify away from the dollar either for yield purposes or to escape US authority. However, what will not happen is that the dollar's share of reserves will fall significantly enough as to see the emergence of a genuinely multipolar currency system, and the reason that it will not happen is due to the lethal combination of capital market scale and capital mobility. As international capital flows now typically involve the transfers of huge amounts of stored quantities of value across financial securities, it follows that few currencies outside of the dollar can withstand the destructive impact of any sudden surges in these flows. In the 1990s, such surges tended to be speculatively driven as certain national currencies perceived to be vulnerable were subjected to attacks by hedge funds and other speculative vehicles. In more recent years, however, these surges have become a regular feature of the global financial landscape as institutionally managed portfolios, having not only grown in scale but also having become more internationally diversified, are highly susceptible to any disturbances in that landscape and therefore need to be readjusted accordingly. The fact that disturbances can now come from any quarter is exemplified by the taper tantrum episode of 2013. In May of that year, Ben Bernanke, the then chair of the Federal Reserve, announced that the Fed would start to wind down its purchases of treasuries that it had been doing as part of its quantitative easing programme that was launched in the wake of the financial crisis of 2007–8. In the event, there was no reduction in the Fed's treasury bond purchases, but the mere announcement to this effect sufficed to spark heavy outflows of funds from EME financial markets with consequent negative impacts on EME sovereign bond yields and currency exchange rates (Hördahl and Shim, 2020).

To counter the negative effects of any sudden surges in portfolio flows, central banks need to hold the bulk of their reserves in assets that combine three attributes regarding their value storage capacity: *safety* (their stored value must hold firm up to the point of sale); *liquidity* (they can be sold quickly without any adverse impact on their price and hence stored value quantity); and, what is also most critical, *scale* (they must be capable of holding such substantial quantities of value as can match those carried in international portfolio flows). Only US treasuries meet all three of these criteria. Other currencies may be backed by safe and liquid government securities, but none have behind them government securities on the scale that the dollar has. As for other asset types that can serve in a reserve capacity, such as cryptocurrencies and digital currencies, these may combine value quantity with liquidity but still fall far short of the safety criterion given that their prices can be highly volatile because subject to sudden shifts in market sentiment. In the end, it is central banks' knowledge that they need at all times to hold a substantial proportion of their reserve portfolios in the form of financial securities that combine safety, liquidity and large value storage capacity that explains why US treasuries have continually accounted for the majority share of all officially held reserves even as their aggregate total has continued to grow exponentially over the last three decades (recall that from $1.7 trillion in 1995, this figure had grown to $13 trillion by 2024). Central banks may well diversify their reserves to include smaller currencies that give better yield than do US treasuries, but this diversification will always remain a development that enhances rather than undermines the current core-satellite structure of officially held reserves where the core is primarily about safety and value quantity storage and the periphery is primarily about yield. There can be no better illustration of this fact than that Canada, Australia, Sweden, South Korea and Singapore, precisely the five countries that are cited by Eichengreen as having currencies that currently serve in an official reserve capacity and that when pooled together might possibly help weaken the US dollar's reserve status, are all themselves major holders of US treasuries.

The situation then, to sum up, is that all of the various advantages that keep the dollar firmly embedded in the dense network of international currency transactions stem, in one way or other, from the huge size gap separating the US capital markets from all other markets. Unless this gap is closed there will be no end to dollar dominance no matter what frontal attempts are made to chip away at the currency transaction network that sustains it. As things currently stand, there are only two areas with the potential to grow their capital markets to a size commensurate with those of the United States – the eurozone and China – and of these two it might seem that China is the one more likely to realize this potential. While the euro retains second place in the international currency hierarchy, its share of daily forex turnover has declined in recent years (from 19 per cent between 2001 and 2010, its share fell to about 16 per cent in 2013 and then to about 15 per cent from that point up to 2022), a decline that has mirrored the eurozone's decline in its percentage share of world financial security volumes (for example, where in 2010 the eurozone's share of the $82.3 trillion worth of bonds then outstanding was 28 per cent as against the US share of 39 per cent, by 2020 its share of the new $123.5 trillion figure had fallen to 20 per cent while the US percentage share continued to remain roughly the same as before [SIFMA, 2023]). By contrast, China's financial markets have grown appreciably in size over the past decade (from 6.5 per cent of world equity stocks in 2012, China's share of these had risen to 11.6 per cent by 2021, and from 4.9 per cent of world's bond stocks in 2012, China's share of these had risen to 17.2 per cent by 2021). Now, while China's capital markets are still smaller than those of the United States by orders of magnitude, China clearly has the economic capacity to go all the way and grow its capital markets to the point where they match those of the United States, thereby putting the renminbi in a position to challenge to the dollar's dominance. The question is whether this is indeed China's real end aim.

All the signs would seem to indicate that China's leadership is serious about challenging the dollar. On the one side, it has steadily promoted the internationalization of the renminbi both through its various trade deals with other governments and through its various international financial support schemes (China's central bank, for example, is currently engaged in currency swaps with over 30 other central banks, a figure twice that of the United States' central bank swaps). On the other side, as a key member of the BRICS association since its foundation, China's government has consistently given vocal support to the alliance's goal of de-dollarizing the global financial system and it now plays a vital role in adding to the various initiatives that are ostensibly aimed at achieving this goal. Examples include the establishment of the Cross-Border Interbank Payment System (Cips), which is intended to rival Chips, the world's largest private sector dollar clearing and settlement system and the Belgium-based SWIFT, and the international launch of the digital renminbi, which allows for transactions to take place without going through Chips or SWIFT. When all of these facts are taken into consideration, it is little wonder that so many commentators believe that it is only a matter of time before the renminbi becomes a serious rival to the dollar. Some commentators, such as Nouriel Rubini, believe that this eventuality will materialize over the next decade, while others believe that it will materialize over a longer period, but what is common to these beliefs is the underlying assumption that China is genuinely interested in seeing its currency rival, if not topple, the dollar as an international currency. In our view, this assumption is wrong because China has no such interest. If China does genuinely want to grow its domestic financial markets to a size comparable to those of the United States, it is not enough that it strengthens its legal and governance infrastructure, lifts all capital mobility restrictions, or adopts any of the other measures designed to attract foreign investor participation in its markets. In the end, what is above all fundamentally necessary is that there be a commitment to full democracy such as can also allow for complete freedom of speech, freedom of the press, freedom to form different political parties and so on. On this crucial issue,

China is not moving forward so much as moving backwards, as attested by the increasing restrictions on Hong Kong's rights as an autonomous region.

While the tightly centralized control exercised by China's ruling Communist Party is not compatible with the full development of China's domestic financial markets, it is on the contrary quite compatible with the Party's aim of securing domestic social stability by securing the foreign markets and foreign resource supplies necessary to maintaining that stability. China currently has a population of over 1.4 billion people, out of which about 780 million are actively engaged in employment. Although this latter figure has fallen in recent years due to demographic change among other factors, it is still a huge workforce when one considers that it is substantially larger than the entire population of the eurozone and over twice the size of the US population of 330 million. To be able to keep this workforce in continual employment, China needs two things. First, it needs to keep labour costs down to maintain export competitiveness, a need that explains why, in the face of rising domestic wages, it is an even more urgent requirement that its central bank maintains the renminbi's exchange rate against the dollar within a target range, a requirement that in turn explains why its central bank continues to hold substantial amounts of US treasuries in its reserves. Second, given the sheer size of its workforce, China has to ensure that there is in place an international resource supply infrastructure of a type that can guarantee the required amounts of resource inflows. To this end, what China currently does across the world is to enter into bilateral agreements with foreign governments whereby in return for its investments in local infrastructure projects or for its other forms of financial assistance it receives priority access to those governments' countries' resources. A good example of this strategy whereby China's bilateral trade and investment agreements with foreign countries effectively lead to much of their resources being taken off the open markets and locked up for the exclusive use of China is the Belt and

Road Initiative launched by President Xi Jinping in 2013. China's encouragement of its EME partners to switch from the use of the dollar to the renminbi in their trade relations with China fits perfectly well into this general scheme of things. Russia and many other allies of China may well believe that the latter is seriously aiming to eventually dethrone the dollar, and China may well encourage this belief or at the very least do nothing to discourage it, but its real end aim in promoting the internationalization of the renminbi is not so much to de-dollarize the global financial system as to help cement foreign resource supply systems to China's industrial base.

A fundamental distinction must be made between China and the eurozone for if China's leadership has no intention of taking the measures necessary to challenging the dollar for the reasons outlined in this chapter, there are some leading bodies in the eurozone that do want to see the euro challenge the dollar and that do understand that the expansion of the eurozone's financial securities markets is vital to this challenge. We have already documented some of the formidable obstacles standing in the way of this expansion and we shall document some more in a later section, but all these obstacles can eventually be overcome providing that there is unanimity of opinion on this issue among all of the eurozone's leaders. This unanimity has so far not been reached but it is just possible that this will now change, the catalyst for this being the United States' increasingly indiscriminate use of the dollar as a political and economic weapon such that US allies in the West can now be victims of this weaponization as much as can its opponents in the East. If there were any lingering illusions to the contrary before Donald Trump's presidency, his presidency ruthlessly destroyed them. Given that Trump means to continue as before during his second term as US president the eurozone's leaders will have to start taking the steps necessary to making the euro strong enough as to be able to give protection against any punitive use of the dollar, which essentially means closing the size gap separating the eurozone's securities markets from those of the United States. Should this happen, those foreign private and official institutional investors already unhappy with the United States' increasing use of the dollar as an economic and political weapon would finally be able to divert substantial amounts of funds away from US securities because they would now have a more viable alternative means of storing their funds. The upshot of what we are saying is that it is not to China but to the eurozone group of countries that countries wanting to challenge the dollar's dominance must look. To put the point another way, if the dividing line in the global trade and production spheres is today between West and East, between the countries grouped around the United States and the countries grouped around China, the dividing line in the global currency sphere should be between West and West, between the currencies clustered around the dollar and the currencies clustered around the euro. This proposition forms the central theme of the third and final part of this book.

PART III

Confronting Dollar Dominance

SIX

How the Euro Can Rival the Dollar

The story of the euro's relation to the dollar in the international currency realm is a story of qualified success, the success lying in the fact that the euro is a strong enough currency to resist the gravitational force of the dollar and the qualification lying in the euro's inability to pull enough of the world's other currencies into its gravitational field as to create a more balanced international currency system. This mixture of success and failure is a direct reflection of the ambivalent size of the eurozone's capital markets: on the one hand large enough to make the euro a regional centre of gravity but on the other hand not large enough to make it a centre of gravity on a par with the dollar in the global arena. While the eurozone's equity markets have lagged behind those of the United States, the lengthening of the size gap separating the euro and the dollar bond markets has been more notable, as attested by the fact that where in 2013 the EU's bond markets accounted for 28.4 per cent of the total world bond volume of $87.7 trillion then outstanding, by 2022 that figure had dropped to 17.3 per cent of the total $129.8 trillion outstanding while the US contribution remained roughly the same at 40 per cent. The closure of the bond market gap must therefore be prioritized if euro–dollar parity is ever to be achieved, and to this end what must be removed are the major obstacles that are holding back the growth rate of the eurozone's bond markets.

One obstacle is the eurozone governments' restrictive stance on public debt, which has to be considerably loosened to bring it into line with that of the US federal government. We shall expand on this particular point after first considering another major obstacle whose removal is more controversial, if not more difficult. This is that the eurozone's corporations' preferred form of external debt funding continues to be heavily weighted towards bank credit unlike the US corporations' preferred form that on the contrary places far greater weight on bond issuance. Simple arithmetic dictates that there should be convergence towards the US corporate debt funding model in order to help close the dollar–euro bond market gap, but the problem that stands in the way here is that the eurozone group of countries are not the only advanced capitalist countries whose corporations lean towards the opposing bank credit model of debt funding. Rather, the list includes the UK, Japan and, indeed, so many other advanced capitalist countries that it is in fact the US model that is the outlier model. This means that if there is to be a good case for convergence, it must first be made independently of the matter of the dollar–euro rivalry in the currency realm; that is to say, it must first be shown that there is a strong economic rationale for convergence regardless of whether it will or will not subsequently help strengthen the euro's international standing. In providing such a rationale in what follows, we begin by challenging an idea that has taken hold since the collapse of communism in the early 1990s, namely, that there can be different varieties of capitalism.

Although there has long been a tradition of comparing different capitalist systems, the collapse of communism brought a noticeable change of focus in that tradition. If a capitalist system is broadly defined as a system of production for the market, then it can be said that prior to communism's collapse the main criterion against which capitalist systems were compared was one that concentrated attention on the *production* side of the production–market nexus. The key questions raised concerned the way in which different institutional structures, labour relation arrangements and policy initiatives served to give capitalist firms a competitive edge at the micro level and capitalist countries a comparative advantage at the macro level.

The change of emphasis following the collapse of communism was that the main comparator criterion became one that foregrounded the *market* side of the production–market nexus, a change exemplified by the 'varieties of capitalism' (VoC) framework that focuses particular attention on differences in the degree to which the market principle is allowed to influence and shape firms' productive activities. From this standpoint, Peter Hall and David Soskice divide capitalist economies into two contrasting types: 'liberal market economies' (LMEs) in which 'market relationships are characterized by the arms-length exchange of goods or services in a context of competition and formal contracting' and 'coordinated market economies' (CMEs) in which 'firms depend more heavily on non-market relationships to coordinate their endeavours with other actors and to construct their core competences' (Hall and Soskice, 2001: 8). If two different types of capitalism are to co-exist, it must be because each type has certain strengths that are unique to it. As concerns the LME type that possesses 'fluid labour and capital markets, which make it easy for firms to begin new ventures knowing that they can quickly be unwound', its main strength is said to be that it offers 'more support for radical innovation, understood as the development of entirely new products or technologies' (Hall, 2015: 5). By contrast, the main strength of the CME type of capitalism characterized by stronger longer-term relations between corporate managers and workers is that it is 'better at incremental innovation, involving quality control and continuous improvements to products or production processes' (Hall, 2015: 5). Now, if the Hall–Soskice VoC line of analysis is correct, there can be no compelling reason why there should be any convergence on the US corporate debt funding model: this model may be appropriate for the United States in that bond finance as a quintessentially arm's-length form of finance is perfectly suited to the LME type of capitalism of which the United States is the exemplar, but it is not suited to the eurozone economies or any other area economies that remain committed to the CME type of capitalism in that this type entails continued commitment to a relational form of corporate financing as exemplified by the bank-credit based corporate debt funding model.

In taking issue with the VoC framework, we do not deny the importance of the locally embedded peculiarities that continue to distinguish capitalist economies. The cultures and customs, and the local rules and traditions, which have historically shaped the various institutional linkages and complementarities in different countries will persist because these are all ultimately essential to the social cohesion that is necessary to the continuity of production. Indeed, it is principally because of this fact that several authors have gone so far as to identify more than two varieties of capitalism.[1] In this respect, we agree with Hall and Soskice that one has to abstract from differing locally embedded customs and traditions and move to a higher level of generalization if one is to bring out the fundamental qualities of capitalism as a generically distinct type of economic system. Where we disagree is that there can be more than one generic type of capitalism. The crux of the matter is that the distinction between the impersonal, arm's-length exchange principle and the associative or relational principle that is used as the criterion for distinguishing between varieties of capitalism is essentially the same criterion that ultimately distinguishes capitalism from all other socio-economic systems. Whatever the many differences separating the previous systems of slavery and feudalism and these systems from the later communist system that flourished for much of the 20th century, what they all had in common was a blanket dominance of the relational principle. There may have been markets in these systems, but what fundamentally sets capitalism apart is not merely that it is a system of production for the market but that market prices are here set according to impersonal and competitively established pricing standards rather than according to any relational forms of price setting. Now if the arm's-length exchange principle is that which fundamentally distinguishes capitalism, it must then follow that as capitalism expands and develops over time so must that principle also expand in its reach and scope accordingly. As we have said, the end of the 20th century marks a watershed in this respect in that if, on the one hand, the globalization of capitalism signified the geographical extension of the arm's-length principle to encompass the entire globe, on the other hand, the financialization of capitalism signified the category extension of that same principle to encompass financial securities inasmuch as the unprecedented growth of their markets could only be made possible with the transformation of equities and bonds into standalone and tradable stores of value and inasmuch as this transformation could only have been made possible on the basis of market sanctioned standards against which securities can be priced at a distance. The upshot of all this is that LME and CME type systems differ not because they represent different varieties of capitalism so much as because they differ in the extent to which they give free reign to the arm's-length principle. Thus, if at one end of the spectrum communism is a system that suppresses this principle everywhere within it, and if at the other end of the spectrum LME capitalism is a system that allows this principle to operate everywhere within it, CME capitalism stands somewhere in the middle of the spectrum in that it restricts the principle in certain areas of its system while allowing it free reign in other areas. In short, LME capitalism, of which the United States is the exemplar, differs from CME capitalism only in the sense that it represents the most logically consistent form of capitalism.

Returning to the difference between the bond-based and bank credit-based corporate debt funding models, the reason why the former has been developed in the United States is that it has a number of functional advantages that arise precisely because of its consistency with the arm's-length exchange principle. The first of these has to do with risk dispersion. All of the world's large corporations tend to rely on a mixture of equity issuance and debt dependence to meet their external funding needs, equities to help share the risks of corporate production with shareholders and debt to avoid too heavy a dilution of ownership rights. This said, the differences in the composition of corporate debt have an important bearing on the extent to which the risk on this debt is dispersed across a host country's financial system. The fact that US corporations rely far more heavily on bonds for their debt funding needs means that any associated risks can be more widely spread across different groups of creditors, whereas the risks of corporate debt funding in countries whose corporations rely more heavily on bank loans is, by that token, concentrated on just one particular group of creditors, namely the banks. Another source of advantage of bond-based corporate debt funding is its greater cost efficiency. As corporate bonds are nothing other than corporate debts compressed into the form of tradable instruments, bond holders do not have be compensated for any loss of liquidity whereas bank creditors must be so compensated given the relational and non-tradable nature of bank loans. Furthermore, the cost differences separating out the US arm's-length corporate debt funding model from other relation-based models are also magnified by the differences in the management of the time profile of debt. The fact that corporations that rely primarily on bank credit for their debt funding needs tend to do so to meet their longer-term needs as much as their shorter-term needs means that the costs of compensating banks for loss of liquidity are for them correspondingly higher. By contrast, US corporations are further helped to contain debt funding costs by the fact that they tend to rely on bank loans only for their short-term funding needs while typically using bonds to meet their longer-term needs. A third advantage of the US corporate debt funding model is its beneficial implications for the balance sheets of US banks: the fact that US corporations rely more heavily on bonds for their longer-term debt funding needs means that US banks have more space to extend credit to a host of other non-corporate clients, whereas there is less space to do the same for those banks whose balance sheets are heavily tied up by extensive loans to their corporate clients.

It was chiefly because of an increasing awareness of the manifold advantages of a bond-based system of corporate debt financing over a bank credit-based system that drove the European Commission to launch its Capital Markets Union (CMU) project in 2015. The rationale behind this choice of route through which to encourage Europe's large corporations to move closer to their US counterparts as regards their debt funding lay in bond market size: by integrating the European Union (EU) member states' bond markets into a single large market, the more will institutional investors be attracted to that market on account of its greater size, depth and liquidity, and the more advantageous, therefore, will be the bond financing terms faced by Europe's corporations. As we know from the widening size gap between the US bond markets and those of the EU, the European Commission has so far failed to make any real headway in shifting Europe's corporations away from their heavy dependence on banks to meet their funding needs. This failure is not due to any loss or weakening of commitment to the CMU initiative. On the contrary, that commitment has continued to be re-affirmed right down to the present time because the lesson first taught by the great financial crisis, and then taught again by the COVID-19 pandemic and Ukraine invasion generated crises, is that a financial system characterized by over-heavy corporate dependence on bank credit that in turn restricts banks' room for manoeuvre is simply not resilient enough to adequately absorb the severe economic repercussions of crises. As the Commission put it in its 2015 document: 'better integrated capital markets would enhance the shock absorbing capacity of the European economy by making it less heavily reliant on banks and thus less vulnerable to a tightening of bank lending' (European Commission, 2015: 4). Rather, the fundamental reason why the CMU project has made so little progress is that there can be no genuine bond market integration unless there is complete harmonization of the various transparency, governance and other institutional standards that are necessary for measuring and comparing the risks to be factored into bond prices, and achieving this task is by no means easy given the deeply entrenched local rules and traditions that distinguish European countries' financial systems. It is in this context that rejection of the idea that there can be two different varieties of capitalism takes on importance because the last thing that the European Commission and other leading bodies in the EU need to hear is that there is no pressing economic imperative for forcing convergence towards the US arm's-length system of corporate finance given that any of this system's strengths can be matched by those possessed by the alternative relation-based system.

As observed, the other major factor behind the slow growth rate of Europe's bond markets as compared to that of the US markets is the European governments' comparatively restrictive stance on government debt. To see the significance of this particular factor to the dollar–euro relation in the international currency sphere one need only look at the US government's large contribution both to the growth volume of total US bonds outstanding (US treasuries accounted for over a quarter of all US securities outstanding at the end of 2022 and have been pivotal to the growth volume of total US securities held by foreign investors [SIFMA, 2023]). Had the eurozone's governments followed the example of their US counterpart over this same period, the euro would have undoubtedly been in a stronger position vis-à-vis the dollar as an international currency, but the fact is that they did not. What is curious about this fact is that, in the years following the financial crisis, the eurozone's governments faced the same highly favourable bond financing terms as did the US government (recall that this was in stark contrast to the financing terms faced by most of the world's emerging market economy governments) and yet, after having bailed out their banks, they chose to execute a sharp policy U-turn and embark on debt-reducing austerity programmes in contrast to the US government that made no such U-turn. What is even more curious is that although it was two US-based economists, Carmen Reinhart and Kenneth Rogoff, that lent academic weight to the case for a post-financial crisis turn to austerity, it was above all the governments of Europe that used this case while that of the United States completely ignored it. Before reviewing the details specifically pertaining to the eurozone governments' turn to austerity in the years following the financial crisis, it is first useful to examine the Reinhart–Rogoff argument that played so influential a role in this period.

The central idea in that argument is that when a government's debt to gross domestic product (GDP) ratio exceeds 90 per cent, the negative consequences for that government's domestic economy can be extremely serious. Underlying this idea of a government debt threshold is the idea of investor debt intolerance: if investors feel that a government has issued too many bonds, they may demand such high interests as compensation against risk as would force the government in question to raise taxes and make substantive expenditure cuts, actions that would in turn squeeze domestic economic growth. Now, while the link running from debt intolerance to a negative impact on growth had long been established in standard macroeconomic theory, what was never established was the exact government debt to GDP ratio at which debt intolerance would kick in and cause substantial damage. Was the tipping point ratio 50 per cent? 100 per cent? 150 per cent? Standard theory never provided an answer, but an answer must be provided, an exact ratio must be specified, if a government that embarks on a deeply unpopular austerity programme aimed at reducing its debt is to be able to counter the public backlash by pointing to the dire consequences of not pursuing such a programme. Reinhart and Rogoff very conveniently produced just such a figure. To quote from their 2010 paper:

> Why are there thresholds in debt, and why 90 per cent? This is an important question that merits further research, but we would speculate that the phenomenon is closely

> linked to [the] logic … of 'debt intolerance' … as debt levels rise towards historical limits, risk premia begin to rise sharply, facing highly indebted governments with difficult tradeoffs. Even countries that are committed to fully repaying their debts are forced to dramatically tighten fiscal policy in order to appear credible to investors and thereby reduce risk premia. (Reinhart and Rogoff, 2010: 23)

In the opening sentence of this paragraph two questions are posed but only one, the first, is answered through an explicit appeal to logic while the second question is left open and only to be subsequently answered through an appeal to the lessons of 200 years of history. Nevertheless, despite the lack of any sound logical grounding to the 90 per cent debt threshold figure, the fact is that it was used to great effect as justification for the post-crisis turn to austerity as was evidenced by the following extract from a speech given in early 2010 by George Osborne who was soon to be the UK's Chancellor of the Exchequer:

> [W]hile private sector debt was the cause of this crisis, public sector debt is likely to be the cause of the next one. As Ken Rogoff himself puts it, 'there's no question that the most significant vulnerability as we emerge from recession is the soaring government debt. It's very likely that will trigger the next crisis as governments have been stretched so wide'. The latest research suggests that once debt reaches more than about 90% of GDP the risks of a large negative impact on long term growth become highly significant. If off-balance sheet liabilities such as public sector pensions are included we are already well beyond that. And even on official internationally comparable measures of debt, we are forecast to break through 90% of GDP in just two years' time. (Osborne, 2010)

Reinhart and Rogoff's extraction of a 90 per cent tipping point ratio from historical experience was subsequently shown to have rested on highly dubious research methods (for a critique of these methods see Herndon et al [2014]). Of more immediate concern here was their premise that this ratio applied equally to all governments that issued debt in their own currencies (the 90 per cent ratio is for governments that borrow in their own currency; for emerging market economy governments that borrow in foreign currencies the ratio is lower at 60 per cent). This premise implies that institutional investors are always free to redirect all of their portfolio funds away from government bonds and towards alternative assets, which is to say that all governments are equally vulnerable to investor debt intolerance. Now if all of this was correct then we should have expected to see the yields on all advanced market economy government bonds rise in tandem with the common rise in the advanced market economy government debt to GDP ratios in the years immediately following the financial crisis of 2007–8. This did not happen. The yields on US treasuries continued to fall even while the US government debt to GDP ratio broke through the 90 per cent threshold figure, and the same was true of the UK's case (see Lysandrou, 2013). As concerns the eurozone, the yields on the bonds of certain weaker eurozone governments rose substantially in this period (the case of Greece and Spain being notable examples), while the yields on the bonds of the stronger eurozone governments continued to fall despite the fact that the 90 per cent threshold figure had been broken through in all cases (Lysandrou, 2013). The explanation for this latter development was that while some of the portfolio funds withdrawn from the bonds of the weaker eurozone governments may have been redirected towards alternative asset classes, the bulk of these funds were instead redirected towards the bonds of the stronger eurozone governments, thus enabling the latter to substantively raise their debt to GDP ratios without incurring negative repercussions. The lesson here, a lesson that was reinforced by the different post-crisis experiences of eurozone governments, is that there cannot be a uniform tipping point of government debt to GDP ratio, whether this be 90 per cent or any other single figure, because when institutional investors are always constrained to hold substantial proportions of their portfolios in the form of government bonds for safety and liquidity reasons, they simply cannot hold up the threat of debt intolerance to all governments at one and the same time. On the contrary, government debt to GDP ratios have to differ across countries because in a context where substantial proportions of portfolio funds must always be contained within the government bond sector, these ratios cannot remain independent of each other but must instead be interdependent inasmuch as one government's low debt to GDP ratio helps to sustain another government's high debt to GDP ratio.

While Reinhart and Rogoff 's 90 per cent threshold figure was particularly influential in promoting a post-financial crisis turn to austerity in the UK, its chief influence in continental Europe lay in helping to reinforce a turn that was already underway due to Germany's insistence. While many governments view their outstanding bonds as nothing other than quantities of debt that have to be kept under tight control, none adheres to this viewpoint more strenuously than does the German government. In its case, certain interpretations of history, together with the continuing weight of moral and cultural attitudes to indebtedness, have produced a fear of issuing government bonds that is little short of pathological. The German government has always made it a priority to maintain a balanced budget over the economic cycle and when forced by circumstances to issue bonds above a given threshold it tries to get back below that threshold as quickly as possible. Just such a pattern was repeated after the financial crisis of 2007–8 when the German government, forced to increase the volume of its debt to finance its various crisis-containing measures, almost immediately sought to reduce this volume through the incorporation of a budgetary correction mechanism or 'debt brake' into the German constitution in 2009. Although the German government was not the first European government to incorporate a debt brake into its constitution (Switzerland, for example, had done so earlier) it was the first to do so in the EU, a fact that was of some importance because it used Germany's position as the most powerful EU economy to persuade as many as possible of the other EU member-state governments to adopt similar debt brakes. Under the force of this persuasion, 25 out of the 27 EU national governments (those of the UK and the Czech Republic having opted out) signed the Fiscal Compact in March 2012, the major terms of which were that the structural budget deficit should not exceed 0.5 per cent of GDP over the medium term and that this arrangement be anchored in the national constitution or on a comparable national legal basis.

In the case of the eurozone group of EU member states, an alternative means of increasing the volume supply of government bonds is through the creation of a common eurozone sovereign bond, that is, a bond jointly guaranteed by all the eurozone member governments. While the idea of such a bond had been floated before the financial crisis of 2007–8, it was only when the scale of the crisis' damaging effects on the eurozone economies became clear that it received serious attention. At the heart of the matter was the crisis' impact on the yield spreads of eurozone government bonds over the German bund. These had converged to the bund following the introduction of the euro because the elimination of currency risk in the eurozone area coupled with the strong growth performance of the eurozone economies and the ensuing confidence in the stability of the eurozone as a whole induced investors to ignore the persisting structural and institutional differences between the eurozone countries and hence also the corresponding differences in sovereign credit risk. However, once the effects of the financial crisis started to take their toll on the eurozone economies and on the finances of the eurozone governments, the issue of sovereign credit risk suddenly became a major source of concern for investors as attested by the sharp divergence in eurozone government yields after 2008. It was against this backdrop that, in November 2011, the European Commission presented a Green Paper in which it argued the case for the introduction of joint government guaranteed eurobonds, or 'stability bonds' as these were labelled, on the grounds that this initiative 'could potentially quickly alleviate the current sovereign debt crisis, as the high-yield Member States could benefit from the stronger creditworthiness of the low-yield Member States' (European Commission, 2011: 2).

Interestingly, when broadening out the case for stability bonds, the European Commission argued that, while on the internal European front 'institutional investors (for example, life insurance companies and pension funds), which tend to hold a relatively high share of domestic sovereign bonds, would benefit from a more homogenous and robust asset in the form of a Stability Bond', on the international front 'Stability Bonds would facilitate portfolio investment in the euro and foster a more balanced global financial system. The larger issuance volumes and more liquid secondary markets implied by Stability Bond issuance would strengthen the position of the euro as an international reserve currency' (European Commission, 2011: 3). None of this had cut any ice with the German government. On the contrary, a number of the 'low-yield Member States' led by Germany strongly objected to the 'stability bond' proposal on two grounds, one to do with the perceived unfairness of debt mutualization (why should their taxpayers be made to help bail out countries that had lived beyond their means?) and the other to do with moral hazard (profligate governments that are continually bailed out would have no incentive to rein in their profligacy). When nearly a decade later, following the global outbreak of the COVID-19 pandemic in early 2020, a number of eurozone governments led by France argued for the issuance of joint government-backed eurobonds, this time labelled 'corona' bonds, to help finance the costs of dealing with the economic and social consequences of the COVID-19 pandemic, the German government, backed by several other northern eurozone governments, again resisted this proposal for the same reasons that they had resisted the earlier 'stability' bond proposal. The one difference was that, on this occasion, Germany agreed to a compromise solution whereby joint eurozone government-backed bonds could be issued as a temporary measure and then only on the strict condition that the funds raised be used solely to finance COVID-19 pandemic recovery programmes.

Germany's opposition to any substantial and permanent expansion of joint eurozone government-backed bonds has negative implications for the eurozone's bond markets as whole not only by depriving these markets of extra quantities of bonds as such but also by depriving them of a robust operational core. Government bonds differ from corporate bonds in essential respects: they represent the safest form of investable asset because governments have the power of taxation and confiscation; this same power means that government bonds are also the archetypal 'information-insensitive' assets, that is, assets which are immune to adverse selection in trading because agents have no need to acquire private information about the current health of the issuer; and the sheer depth of the markets for government bonds means that these typically represent the most liquid type of assets. These factors explain why government bonds are generally used as the benchmarks against which the risks on all other securities are priced, why they are the dominant constituents in the bond market indexes that are widely used by institutional investors for bond portfolio management purposes, and why commercial banks and asset managers are required to hold substantial amounts of these bonds in their portfolios for regulatory or prudential reasons. Government bonds are also of key importance to the bond markets via their importance to the short-term money markets. Large, deep and liquid bond markets can only exist with the aid of various support services, and these services can in turn only be provided on the scale and with the efficiency required if brokers, dealers and other financial institutions are able to borrow and lend cash and securities in whatever volumes and with whatever frequencies are necessary. While a minority of these borrowing and lending transactions take an unsecured form, the great majority involve the use of collateral in order to minimize counterparty risk and the most superior forms of collateral are government bonds. With these points in mind, it is easy to see that what helps to pull the different types of US securities together into a structured compact mass is the fact that this mass always has a large supply of US treasuries at its core (in 2022, for example, the US government and its agencies accounted for over a quarter of the $90 trillion worth of US debt and equity securities then outstanding [SIFMA, 2023]). Furthermore, it is easy to see that one of the principal reasons why the growth rates of the eurozone's securities markets have lagged behind those of the US markets over the past two decades is that where the latter are served by abundant supplies of US treasuries the former have in contrast been starved of sovereign bonds, whether sole government-backed or joint government-backed, for reasons that are chiefly if not exclusively due to the German government's pathological attitude to government debt.

From all that has been said here, there are clearly many formidable barriers that are preventing the euro from closing the gap with the dollar as an international currency. Nevertheless, the barriers are not insuperable. What in the first place gives cause for this optimistic standpoint is that while other groups of countries in other areas of the world had in the past given serious thought to forming regional currency unions but never succeeded in doing so because of the immense difficulties, the eurozone group of countries succeeded in pressing ahead with their currency union despite the difficulties. What is even more remarkable is that having initially planned for a small euro area to begin with, what actually emerged was a large euro area from the outset that meant that the success of the whole euro project had to surmount an even greater range of difficulties. The euro's origins hold important lessons for today, for if the euro area was suddenly expanded beyond what was initially planned to factor in newly unfolding developments in the global economic and political landscape, so can a further strengthening of the euro's international standing now also occur because there are now also new developments in the global landscape that call for just such a strengthening. Chief among these new developments is the United States' readiness to use the dollar as an economic and political weapon against its European allies because it is those in the euro area that are most vulnerable to the weaponization of the dollar. Where in the case of Russia and other emerging market economy countries, the United States' principle financial weapon is to shut these countries out of any dollar-based international clearing and settlement systems, its principal weapon in the case of the eurozone countries could conceivably be the termination of the central bank swap arrangements between the US Federal Reserve and the European Central Bank (ECB). These arrangements began on a temporary basis in 2011 following the financial crisis and were then made permanent in 2015, but they are far from being symmetrically balanced because the fact that European commercial banks hold dollar assets that are far in excess of the euro assets held by US commercial banks means that the ECB's dependence on the dollars supplied by the Federal Reserve is far greater than is the latter's dependence on the euros supplied by the ECB. It thus follows that should the Federal Reserve cut off its dollar supplies to the ECB, the negative impact on the European banking sector would be immense. Now the Federal Reserve is supposed to conduct its policies independently of any interference from the US government, but can the ECB and the eurozone group of countries more generally really afford to put this independence to the test in an era when there is always uncertainty as to the type of individual that holds the office of US president? The answer is surely no, and it is for this reason that there may now be an acceleration of the European capital market union project and of other associated policy measures such as are needed to give the euro enough international weight as can allow it to rival dollar power.

SEVEN

Why the Euro Must Rival the Dollar

If the euro's international position was to be strengthened to the point where it rivals the dollar, the major benefit to the eurozone area is that it would be made more immune to any adverse use of dollar power. But what would be the wider benefits of a bipolar international currency system? How would the world as a whole gain from having a more balanced, more symmetrical international currency system? A number of highly plausible answers could be given to this question, but the one that will be advanced here as a starting point is that a greatly strengthened euro will make it easier for a global wealth tax to see the light of day. If it is asked why this particular motive for challenging the dollar's dominance should be first singled out, the simple answer is that the principal factors that today underpin that dominance are essentially the same as those that underpin today's unprecedented degree of global wealth concentration. If it is then asked how strengthening the euro could possibly facilitate a global wealth tax policy, the answer is that it would do so by giving that policy a better than zero chance of realization. In the absence of any counterweight power to that of the dollar, a global wealth tax would have absolutely no chance of ever being introduced because it would disproportionately impact the United States' very wealthy individuals given the disproportionate degree to which these individuals dominate the global wealth pyramid. No one, of course, should be under any illusion that a stronger euro will automatically translate into a stronger prospect of a global wealth tax. On the contrary, there will still be substantial hurdles standing in its way, not least because of fierce opposition from the wealthy individuals spread across the eurozone member countries. Nevertheless, whatever the hurdles, the fact remains that any move away from a dollar-centred international currency system towards a bipolar one will at least improve the chance of a global wealth tax. In spelling out some reasons for capitalizing on that chance we begin with some data regarding global wealth concentration.

For this data, we draw on that provided by the Capgemini Research Institute in its annual world wealth report, a publication that dates back to 1996. While recognizing that this data cannot be completely accurate given much of the secrecy that shrouds private wealth concentration, it can nevertheless be considered to give a reasonably accurate picture of the major trends in this concentration. In 2021, the world's high net worth individuals (HNWIs), that is, individuals with assets net of primary residence of $1 million and above, totalled 21.7 million and held approximately $86 trillion worth of assets (Capgemini, 2022). A fact even more striking than the total amount of HNWI wealth is its hugely unequal distribution within the HNWI population. Thus, where the ordinary millionaires (those holding between $1 million and $5 million worth of assets), numbering 19.5 million (90 per cent of the HNWI population), held 43 per cent of the total estimated HNWI assets in 2021, and where the mid-tier millionaires (those holding between $5 million and $30 million worth of assets), numbering 1.9 million, held 22.7 per cent of those estimated assets, the super-HNWIs (those holding over $30 million worth of assets), numbering just 210,000, held 34 per cent of those assets, that is to say, assets worth approximately $28 trillion. The clue to this massive concentration of wealth at the very top of the global wealth pyramid lies in the category breakdown of the assets in which wealth is stored. The sources of wealth origination are many, but there are basically only five asset categories in which wealth is stored – cash, equities, bonds, real estate, alternative investments (that is, investments in hedge funds, private equity, and so on) – and of these five it is the financial securities categories of equities and bonds that between them account for an average of around 50 per cent of total HNWI wealth holdings. When we add this latter observation to the more general observation that over the past three decades or so the growth rates of world equity and bond volumes have considerably outstripped the growth rate of world gross domestic product (GDP), we can understand how the financialization of the global economy lies at the root not only of global wealth concentration but also of the concentration within that concentration: once wealth is originated and any surplus that is not consumed stored in income-generating financial assets, that wealth accumulates of its own accord with the result that the greater the amount of wealth held, the greater the rate of wealth accumulation, which then helps to explain the widening gaps separating the different groups of HNWIs.

In one important sense, the massive degree of global wealth concentration makes it comparatively easier to impose a global wealth tax because all that is required as a first step in this direction is to target the 210,000 or so super-HNWIs. As stated, this small group of wealthy individuals held about $28 trillion of assets in 2021. Assuming, as a conservative estimate, that these assets generated an average return of about 5 per cent in that year, then the super-HNWIs would have earned about $1.4 trillion, a sum roughly on a par with the 2021 GDP figure for Brazil or for Russia but above the corresponding figures for many other large economies such as, for example, Spain and Australia. It follows from this assumption that even with the imposition of a very moderate wealth tax on the super-HNWIs, the amounts of funds that could be generated and made available for distribution to the world's benefit would be very substantial. The urgent need to help the world's poorest counties tackle climate change illustrates the point. At the 2009 COP 15 conference held in Copenhagen, it was agreed that the world's wealthier countries would contribute $100 billion a year to the poorer countries to help them adopt the necessary measures for climate change mitigation and adaptation, but in no year up to 2022 was that target met. If, for example, we take the ten years following the 2009 agreement, we find that the average annual amount of climate change funds raised over that period was around $70 billion. By contrast, a small tax, of say 10 per cent, imposed on the annual incomes of the world's 210,000 ultra-wealthy individuals would comfortably generate that $100 billion.

Whatever may be the benefits to society of a global wealth tax, the fact remains that a solid case for this tax can never be made unless it is also shown that excessive global wealth concentration can have serious harmful consequences for the global economy. In this regard, the question of whether the world's super-wealthy individuals played any causal role in the financial crisis of 2007–8 assumes particular importance given the scale of that crisis' destructive economic impact. The answer to this question has been generally negative. Even Thomas Piketty, who it is fair to say has recently done more than any other individual in getting a global wealth tax placed on the discussion agenda if not on the policy one, concurred with this negative answer when stating in his 2014 book, *Capital in the 21st Century*, that wealth concentration 'was not the sole or even primary cause of the financial crisis' (Piketty, 2014: 298). This position is of course entirely compatible with those explanations of the financial crisis that attribute its root cause to failures within the banking sector. From this vantage point, the only aspect of economic inequality that had any direct causal bearing on the financial crisis was that which concerned the very poorest US households that took out mortgages that they simply could not afford. As Raghuram Rajan argued in his 2010 book, *Fault Lines*, in addition to the US commercial banks that used residential mortgage loans as the principal raw material for creating collateralized debt obligations (CDOs), the other two major groups that were complicit in the expansion of these toxic securities to levels that eventually proved fatal were the US households that took out the subprime and other non-conforming mortgage loans in the first place and the US government authorities that encouraged the securitization of these loans as a supposedly efficient means of expanding US home ownership.

As it was the collapse of the CDO market that triggered the financial crisis, it obviously follows that the causal role played by the world's HNWIs in the crisis drops out of view in explanations of the pre-crisis growth of the CDO market that give primacy to the regulatory arbitrage activities of the banks and only assign investors a secondary, if not entirely passive, role as the buyers of CDOs. On the contrary, the importance of the HNWIs' role comes very clearly into view in explanations of the financial crisis that reverse the equation and instead see the banks as having stepped up their pre-crisis rate of supply of CDOs and other mortgage-backed securities largely in response to the investor asset demand pressures spilling over from the other US debt securities markets.[1] The number of HNWIs was around 10 million in 2007, a figure that represented just 0.15 per cent of the world's population of 6.6 billion. The supposition that these individuals could have had any significant impact in the US bond markets in the years leading up to the financial crisis era may seem incredible when one considers how small in number they were, but not when one considers the amount of wealth that they concentrated in their hands and the forms in which this wealth was stored. In 2007 the world's HNWIs had approximately $41 trillion in assets (world GDP in that year was $55 trillion) as compared with approximately $19 trillion in 1997, which is to say that at the time of the financial crisis, HNWIs were the single largest global investor group with more assets under management than pension funds ($28 trillion), mutual funds ($26 trillion) and insurance companies ($20 trillion). Financial securities were the most dominant type of assets in which HNWIs stored their wealth, accounting for an average of 54 per cent for the period 2002 to 2007. Given that HNWI asset allocation to bonds alone accounted for $11 trillion in 2007 (roughly 14 per cent of the total global stock of bonds in that year) and that around a half of this sum was allocated to US bonds, including US corporate bonds and US government-backed mortgage bonds (agency bonds) in addition to US treasuries, HNWIs exerted a negative influence on US bond yields by virtue of their 'blocking' role: amounts of HNWI US bond holdings were so substantial that had these amounts been available to all of the other groups of large investors the US bond quantity shortage problem and the corresponding problem of yield would not have been as acute as they were and the pressure on the banking sector to step up the supply rate of private label mortgage-backed products would not have been as great as it was.

Aside from the HNWIs' direct contribution to the causal origins of the financial crisis, there was also their indirect contribution made via the hedge funds.[2] Hedge fund assets more than tripled between 2003 and 2007, rising from $600 billion to about $2.2 trillion, while the number of firms operating within the industry doubled from about 5,000 to about 10,000 in this period (Lysandrou, 2012). The two principal sources of the funds injected into the hedge funds over this short time span were the pension funds and other institutional investors, whose overall percentage share contribution to the hedge fund assets base rose from under 2 per cent in 2002 to about 50 per cent by 2007, and the HNWIs that still remained the largest single group of investors in hedge funds despite the decline in their percentage share of these investments (Goda and Lysandrou, 2014). Faced with these large cash inflows from institutional and private clients demanding extra yield, the hedge funds found that one of the most effective ways of meeting this demand was through buying CDOs, precisely the type of financial products that could provide high yield on account of the high risk attaching to them. There should never have been a market for these toxic subprime mortgaged-backed securities given that their complex and opaque structure made it difficult for them to be accurately valued and priced according to any market standard. Yet, as already noted, outstanding CDO volumes grew 12-fold from $0.25 trillion to $3 trillion between 2003 and mid-2007 and they did so in large part because of the hedge funds who were able to use both their financial expertise and their freedom from any risk control constraints to invest heavily in CDOs. There were other notable CDO buyers, such as the European commercial banks, that used these products as collateral for the short-term securities (ABCP) that they sold to the US money market mutual funds, but even their 26 per cent share of the $3 trillion worth of CDO holdings in 2007 fell far short of the hedge funds' 46 per cent share (Lysandrou, 2012). Charles Goodhart, in an article published in 2008 shortly after the outbreak of the financial crisis conjectured that: 'The trigger for the crisis was, as everyone knows, the rising defaults in the US sub-prime mortgage market, but … the trigger could have been almost anywhere else' (Goodhart, 2008: 3). This conjecture may or may not be plausible, and we lean to the latter position, but the indisputable fact remains that it was the sudden collapse of the market for subprime-backed CDOs in August 2007 that spread the fear and panic on a scale sufficient to threaten the complete collapse of the global financial system. In the end, it is because of this fact that the role played by the world's HNWIs in the financial crisis had to have been of pivotal importance given not only that these individuals had helped to cause a US bond shortage and corresponding yield problem through their substantial US bond holdings but also that they had helped to cause the expansion of the CDO market to crisis-threatening proportions through their substantial investments in the hedge funds.

When turning to the COVID-19 pandemic generated crisis of 2020–1, we obviously have to view any connection with global wealth concentration from the reverse angle that tracks the crisis' impact on the scale of that concentration. The picture that emerges from this angle is truly disturbing. In 2020, the total estimated amount of HNWI wealth was $79.6 trillion, a $5.6 trillion increase over the 2019 figure of $74 trillion. That total rose again in 2021 to $86 trillion, an increase of $6.4 trillion over the previous year's figure. Over these same two COVID-19-stricken years, nominal world GDP fell to $85.11 trillion in 2020 as compared with the 2019 figure of $87.65 trillion before subsequently rising to $96.51 trillion in 2021. In short, while the global economy was badly hit by the COVID-19 pandemic, only registering an overall increase in world GDP of $8.9 trillion over 2020–1, world HNWI wealth had by contrast risen by the substantially larger amount of $12 trillion over this same two-year period. A further notable point is that while over 2020–1 HNWI wealth had increased across all three categories of the HNWI population as classified according to the respective amounts of net wealth held, the rate of increase was highest in the ultra-HNWI category. These facts serve to give perfect illustration of the parasitic nature of global wealth ownership, and particularly that of the super-HNWIs at the top of the global wealth pyramid, because, without these individuals having to do anything, their wealth was bound to increase significantly over the 2020–1 period given that much of it was stored in financial securities and given that the prices of these securities were bound to automatically rise in tandem with the expansion of the public expenditure and quantitative easing programmes aimed at containing the destructive effects of the COVID-19 pandemic. Although the central bank authorities were well aware that their monetary policies had beneficial side-effects for the world's super-rich individuals, their common response was that regrettable as were these side-effects, it was not in their policy remit to do anything about them. Now, were it the case that a global wealth tax was in operation in 2020–1, it could have served as an important corrective mechanism, taking some of the HNWI's unearned incomes generated by the COVID-19 crisis-containing policy measures and channelling the resulting funds back into the stricken global economy. However, strong opposition to a global wealth tax has ensured that it has yet to become reality and nowhere is that opposition stronger than in the United States.

In addition to data regarding the volume growth of HNWI-held wealth, Capgemini's world wealth reports also provide data regarding the breakdown of the HNWI population according to nationality. The image that immediately strikes one when looking at the tables containing this data is that of a steep ski slope, with US-based HNWIs occupying sole position at the very top of the slope, HNWIs from two or three other countries occupying a mid-slope position, and the world's other HNWIs spread more or less evenly along the slope's bottom stretch. Capgemini's world wealth reports have appeared annually from 1996 down to the present day and while over this period there have been some changes in the mid and bottom sections of the ski slope, what has never changed is the top position occupied by US HNWIs. The fundamental reason why the United States has consistently accounted for over 30 per cent of the world's HNWI population over the last three decades, while at the same time accounting for under 3 per cent of the world's total population, lies in the financialization of the world economy that has unfolded at an unprecedented rate over this period. Let us recall that although there are many sources of wealth origin, there are basically only five types of assets in which surplus HNWI wealth is stored, and while virtually all areas of the world contribute to the supplies of three of these asset types – cash, real estate and alternative investments – the supplies of the remaining two types, equities and bonds, are heavily dominated by the United States. Now, if we add the observation that the United States on average accounts for around 40 per cent of the world's equity and bond volumes to the observation that HNWIs on average store around 50 per cent of their wealth in equities and bonds it then obviously follows that it is US HNWIs that must benefit the most from the increasing scale asymmetry between the world's financial securities markets and the world's product markets. Nothing better illustrates this point than that it was both the numbers of US HNWIs and the amounts of their wealth holdings that were given the greatest boost by the COVID-19 crisis-containing policies pursued over 2020–1 (thus, of the $12 trillion increase in global HNWI over this two-year period, nearly one half of this amount, $5.4 trillion, went to US HNWIs [Capgemini, 2022]). In the end, it is the United States' preponderate share of the world's HNWI population and wealth holdings that places a formidable obstacle in the way of a global wealth tax, because if on the one hand that tax can never be made workable unless US HNWIs are brought under its umbrella, on the other hand the likely disproportionate impact of a global wealth tax on those individuals means that they will always use their power and influence over the United States' two major political parties to ensure that this tax never gets placed on the policy agenda.

Apart from defending the interests of US HNWIs, US governments will have their own motives for objecting to a global wealth tax. The point at issue here is that for this tax to be operational it needs to be administered by an authority with powers to monitor and enforce it on a globally coordinated basis, and the establishment of such an authority would portend a radical change in the current global institutional architecture. As things currently stand, the only global institutions that have any connection to the running of the global economy are either those that set down and umpire common standards and rules of conduct (the Bank for International Settlements in the sphere of banking or the World Trade Organization in the sphere of trade are two examples) or that provide countries with heavily conditioned financial assistance to help them function in line with prevailing standards and rules of conduct (the International Monetary Fund and the International Bank for Reconstruction and Development are notable examples). What is now needed, however, are global institutions that are equipped with the same interventionist powers of correction and redistribution as have national governments. We previously noted that while the successive major crises engulfing global capitalism over recent decades have impacted all of its member states to one degree or other, the ability with which they have been able to cope with these destructive impacts has varied considerably. This is not all, for, as has also been noted, the reverse side of the fact that countries' abilities to cope with crises now vary in proportion to the size, depth and hence crisis-absorption power of their domestic financial markets is that one country's crisis-containing actions can seriously hamper the actions taken by other countries. It is these observations that now give justification to the creation of entirely new global public institutions armed with powers that do not usurp those of national governments so much as complement them in ways that either reinforce any internationally beneficial effects of these governments' policy actions or that offset any internationally detrimental effects. The problem is that no US government is going to accept any such radical change to the current global institutional status quo because this serves it extremely well, and it does so courtesy of its currency. The dollar's dominant position in the international currency hierarchy places a US government in a corresponding position to champion radical global institutional change, but the paradox is that that same dominant position of the dollar is precisely that which gives any US government cause to resist any such institutional change.

The logic here turns on the way that both the commanding scale of the US financial markets relative to other financial markets and the commanding scale of the dollar's dominance over other national currencies lock together in a reciprocally reinforcing relationship: where it is the scale asymmetry separating the US markets from other markets that continually reinforces the dollar's dominance, this dominance in turn continually reinforces that scale asymmetry. The US government's treasury bonds are central to this reciprocity, for where on one side the increasing issuing rate of these bonds is one of the key drivers behind the scale growth of the US securities markets that continually empowers the dollar, on the reverse side it is the continuing empowerment of the dollar that then facilitates the US government's ability to issue more bonds on a cost-efficient basis as foreign investors demand more of these bonds for one dollar-linked purpose or other. Global crises and ensuing disorder further strengthen this scenario as foreign portfolio investors flee to the safety of US securities and foreign central banks increase their use of US treasuries to mitigate any adverse exchange rate effects arising out of that flight to safety. We saw in the discussion on the COVID-19 pandemic's global impact how the US social services sector benefits considerably from the US government's ability to borrow vast sums comparatively cheaply. However, another sector that also benefits considerably is the military sector. It is illustrative of this point that in 2022 the US government spent $775 billion on arms expenditure, a sum that amounted to about 40 per cent of the world's $2.1 trillion military expenditure for that year, or, to put it another way, a sum that was equal to the combined sum spent by the next ten highest military spending governments (SIPRI, 2023). The fact that the US government could do this without any increase in domestic taxation is of course in large part due to the willingness of central banks to hold trillions of its treasury bonds that yield comparatively low returns. This fact, combined with the fact that the United States is also by far the world's leading exporter of military weaponry (for example, it accounted for an average of 40 per cent of all international arms transfers between 2018 and 2022), shows how much the United States is completely parasitic on the global economy in that it not only takes out from that economy more than it puts back in but also that much of what it does put back in is aimed at shielding its parasitism. This observation points to the major reason why it remains the case that the only global institutions with any connection to the running of the global economy have a very limited remit: it is simply not in the US government's interests to allow any widening of that remit beyond an umpiring role and, as the chief financial backer of these global institutions (something which yet again owes much to the US government's ability to borrow vast sums from its international creditors), it has the voting power to veto any policy proposal to the contrary. This is where the need for a euro with strong enough power to match that of the dollar enters the picture, for while current global institutional arrangements suit the interests of the United States, they most certainly do not suit those of the world taken as a whole.

A global tax authority charged with enforcing a global wealth tax will have to be introduced sooner or later because there are now economic reasons for introducing this tax that are as compelling as any moral ones. The world will simply not be able to continue to function normally when the overwhelming majority of its nearly eight billion people remain mired in poverty while at the other end of the spectrum 200,000 super-rich individuals earn more annual incomes from their stored wealth than do the great majority of the world's 195 nation states. To say that a strong euro is a necessary prerequisite for radical change in the current global institutional arrangements is by no means to ignore or downplay the formidable opposition to any such change that will come from the HNWIs spread across the eurozone area. Nevertheless, the fact that the euro is shared by many countries, some of which have electable political parties that span a wide stretch of the political spectrum, makes it more possible for radical policy proposals to be made because the power of HNWIs in the euro area is more dispersed and hence more diluted than it is in either of the world's other two major economies, the United States and China. France's wealth tax from 1981 to 2018 (the 'solidarity wealth tax') is a case in point. This policy ultimately failed because the ease with which HNWIs can move both themselves and their wealth across borders means that no wealth tax that targets ultra-rich individuals can work unless operated on a globally coordinated basis. This said, the fact remains that a leading member state of the European Union, and then also of euro area, actually experimented with a wealth tax, which is something that will simply not happen in the United States and nor, for that matter, in China. The United States and China are in many essential respects polar opposites, one being democratic and allowing a complete range of freedoms, while the other is undemocratic and allows few freedoms, but what both countries have in common is an exceptionally high degree of political power and wealth concentration: where the United States has only two electable political parties that are both heavily financed by its HNWIs, China has one political party that is staffed by leaders that are either members of, or have close connections with, China's HNWI population that in terms of size stands somewhere in the middle of the world HNWI geographical ski slope. As with the US government, the Chinese government has no desire to see the formation of new types of global institutional authorities that have powers to interfere in its domestic arrangements or in its international operations and, as with the US government, it will always oppose any global wealth tax not only because of the need to defend the interests of its HNWIs but also because it too fully understands that to allow this policy measure through is to open the door to other policy measures that would require the establishment of other similar types of interventionist global authorities.

Outside of the eurozone, there are many other countries in the world with a similar degree of political plurality that allow calls for radical policies and for radical institutional change to be made, but none of these countries have the power to leverage up international support for these calls because, in the current era of financialization, power ultimately means currency power and none of them have this type of power. It is because the eurozone is unique in that it is a regional area comprising of many countries with many political parties while also having just one common currency that explains why it is in the best position to lead calls for radical change. This is not to say that the eurozone is about to make these calls any time soon. Indeed, the contrary is the case not least because, as things currently stand, the electoral sway of political parties that are pushing forward highly populist and divisive policy agendas is as marked across many parts of the eurozone as it is elsewhere. Yet, while this is the situation today across the eurozone, the situation may possibly change tomorrow as political parties pushing forward unifying and progressive policies again gain ascendency, and it is this possibility that explains why the international role of the euro must be considerably strengthened. In the end, what we are saying is that when at some point in the future it becomes obvious that the world's national governments will no longer be able to contain the manifold destructive effects of increasing global economic inequality and that any realistic hope of dealing with those effects requires the creation of a new global institutional architecture, a strong euro with enough international power that can match that of the dollar offers the best chance of meeting that requirement.

Notes

one Financialization and the Gravitational Force of the Dollar

1 Currencies' percentage shares of daily forex turnover are calculated out of 200 per cent because each currency pair is counted twice, but here we divide these percentages by two to make them comparable to other percentage ratios that will be referred to.

2 See, for example, Epstein (2005) or Van der Zwan (2014).

3 For a recent overview of the heterodox approach of financialization, see Sawyer (2022). For an earlier critique of this approach, see Lysandrou (2016).

4 For further discussion of financialization as the colonization of the future, see Lysandrou (2016).

5 From an average percentage share of government expenditure of just 8 per cent in 1960, that share had risen to an average of 17 per cent across the OECD countries by 1990 and to an average of 20 per cent in 2018. The average share for the EU-28 countries in 2018 was 40 per cent, but closer to 50 per cent for the UK and other northern European countries, a figure similar to that for the United States (OECD, 2019a).

6 Governments could finance most of their expenditure out of tax income because up to the 1930s this expenditure averaged 10 per cent of GDP whereas today it averages nearly 50 per cent. See Tanzi (1999) and Tanzi and Schuknecht (2000).

7 For further detail on this point see, for example, Forbes (2010) or Darvas and Hüttl (2017).

two Resisting the Dollar's Gravitational Force: The Euro's Rationale Revisited

1 Much of this chapter draws on Lysandrou and Stassinopoulos (2020).

2 See, for example, De Grauwe (2013a).

3 See, for example, Wheatley (2013) and Germain and Schwartz (2014).

4 Quoted by Rinaldi and Santini (1998: 92).

5 See, for example, Germain and Schwartz (2014).

three The Financial Crisis of 2007–8

1 See Lysandrou and Shabani (2018); Lysandrou et al (2020); Lysandrou (2022) for a fuller account of this storyline.

2 See Minsky (1977; 1982; 1986).

six How the Euro Can Rival the Dollar

1 See, for example, Whitley (1999), Amable (2003) and Becker (2009).

seven Why the Euro Must Rival the Dollar

1 This line of argument was put in Goda and Lysandrou (2014). See also Lysandrou (2019).

2 For a full account of the hedge funds' role in the subprime crisis see Lysandrou (2012).

References

Alami, I. and Dixon, A. (2020) State capitalism(s) redux? Theories, tensions, controversies, *Competition & Change*, 24(1): 70–94.

Alami, I., Dixon, A., Gonzalez-Vicente, R., Babic, M., Lee, S.-O., Medby, I.A. and De Graaff, N. (2022) Geopolitics and the 'new' state capitalism, *Geopolitics*, 27(3): 995–1023.

Amable, B. (2003) *The Diversity of Modern Capitalism*, Oxford: Oxford University Press.

Bank of England (2007a) *Financial Stability Report*, April.

Bank of England (2007b) *Financial Stability Report*, October.

Becker, U. (2009) *Open Varieties of Capitalism: Continuity, Change and Performance*, np: Palgrave Macmillan.

BIS (Bank for International Settlements) (2022) *Triennial Survey of the Foreign Exchange and OTC Derivatives Markets in 2022*, November.

Borio, C. (2014) The international monetary and financial system: its Achilles heel and what to do about it, Working Paper No. 456, Bank for International Settlements.

Buzan, B. (2011) A world order without superpowers: decentred globalism, *International Relations*, 25(1): 3–25.

Buzan, B. and Lawrence, G. (2014) Capitalism and the emergent world order, *International Affairs*, 90(1): 71–91.

Caballero, R.J. (2010) The 'other' imbalance and the financial crisis, NBER Working Paper No. 15636, January.

Capgemini (2022) *World Wealth Report 2022*.

Carney, M. (2018) True finance: ten years after the financial crisis. Speech given at the Economic Club of New York, 19 October.

Chinn, M. and Frankel, J. (2008) Why the euro will rival the dollar, *International Finance*, 11(1): 49–73.

Cohen, B.J. (2009) Towards a leaderless currency system. In *The Future of the Dollar*, edited by E. Helleiner and J. Kirshner. London: Cornell University Press, pp 140–159.

Darvas, Z. and Hüttl, P. (2017) Returns on foreign assets and liabilities: exorbitant privileges and stabilizing adjustments, Bruegel Working Paper 07, November.

De Grauwe, P. (2013a) The political economy of the euro, *Annual Review of Political Science*, 16(1): 153–170.

De Grauwe, P. (2013b) Design failures in the eurozone: can they be fixed? *European Economy Economic Papers*, 491/April.

de Silguy, Y.T. (1997) The euro and the Asian financial markets. *Conference Euromoney/AUME*, Hong Kong, 23 September, speech/97/187.

Eichengreen, B. (2022) Ukraine war accelerates the stealth erosion of dollar dominance, *Financial Times*, 28 March.

Epstein, G. (ed) (2005) *Financialization and the World Economy*, Cheltenham: Edward Elgar.

European Commission (1990) One market, one money: an evaluation of the potential benefits and costs of forming an economic and monetary union. *European Economy*, No. 44, October.

European Commission (1997) External aspects of economic and monetary union, *Euro Papers*, 1 July.

European Commission (2011) Green paper on the feasibility of introducing stability bonds, COM (2011) 818 final, Brussels, 23 November.

European Commission (2015) Green paper: building a capital markets union, COM (2015) 63 final, Brussels, 18 February.

Financial Times Editorial Team (2023) Threats to the dollar's dominance are overblown, *Financial Times*, 19 April.

Flassbeck, H. and Lapavitsas, C. (2015) *Against the Troika: Crisis and Austerity in the Eurozone*, London and New York: Verso.

Forbes, K.J. (2010) Why do foreigners invest in the United States, *Journal of International Economics*, 80(1): 3–21.

Fratianni, M. (1998) Maxi versus mini EMU: the political economy of stage III, *Columbia Journal of European Law*, 4(2): 375–393.

Galbraith, J. (2022) A multipolar financial world is here, *Institute for New Economic Thinking (INET)*, 5 May.

Germain, R. and Schwartz, H. (2014) The political economy of failure: the euro as an international currency, *Review of International Political Economy*, 21(5): 1095–1122.

Goda, T. and Lysandrou, P. (2014) The contribution of wealth concentration to the subprime crisis: a quantitative estimation, *Cambridge Journal of Economics*, 38: 301–327.

Goodhart, C.A.E. (2008) The background to the 2007 financial crisis, *International Economics and Economic Policy*, 4(4): 331–346.

Grahl, J. and Lysandrou, P. (2017) Germany's brake on European capital-market development, *European Journal of Economics and Economic Policies: Intervention*, 15(3): 364–381.

Group of Ten (1993) *International Capital Movements and Foreign Exchange Markets: Report to the Ministers and Governors by the Group of Deputies*, Basel: Bank for International Settlements.

Hall, P.A. (2015) Varieties of capitalism. In *Emerging Trends in the Social and Behavioural Sciences*, edited by R. Scott and S. Kosslyn. Hoboken: John Wiley & Sons, pp 1–15.

Hall, P. and Soskice, D. (2001) *Varieties of Capitalism*, Oxford: Oxford University Press.

Herndon, T., Ash, M. and Pollin, R. (2014) Does high public debt consistently stifle economic growth? A critique of Reinhart and Rogoff, *Cambridge Journal of Economics*, 38(2): 257–279.

Hördahl, P. and Shim, I. (2020) EME bond portfolio flows and long-term interest rates during the Covid-19 pandemic, *BIS Bulletin*, No. 18, May.

Ikenberry, G.J. (2024) Three worlds: the west, east and south and the competition to shape global order, *International Affairs*, 100(1): 121–138.

IMF (International Monetary Fund) (2024) *Currency Composition of Official Foreign Exchange Reserves (COFER)*, September.

Lysandrou, P. (2012) The primacy of the hedge funds in the subprime crisis, *Journal of Post Keynesian Economics*, 34(2): 225–253.

Lysandrou, P. (2013) Debt intolerance and the 90% debt threshold: two impossibility theorems, *Economy and Society*, 42(4): 521–542.

Lysandrou, P. (2016) The colonisation of the future: an alternative view of financialisation and its portents, *Journal of Post Keynesian Economics*, 39(4): 444–472.

Lysandrou, P. (2019) *Commodity: The Global Commodity System in the 21st Century*, London: Routledge.

Lysandrou, P. (2022) The European Banks' role in the financial crisis of 2007–8: A critical assessment, *New Political Economy*, 27(5): 879–894.

Lysandrou, P. and Shabani, M. (2018) The explosive growth of the US ABCP market between 2004 and 2007: a search for yield story, *Journal of Post Keynesian Economics*, 41(4): 526–546.

Lysandrou, P. and Stassinopoulos, Y. (2020) Resisting the gravitational pull of the dollar: the economic rationale behind a large Eurozone, *Economy and Society*, 49(3): 387–405.

Lysandrou, P., Shabani, M. and D'Avola, C. (2020) The explosive growth of the US ABCP market between 2004 and 2007: an integrated empirical analysis, *Quarterly Review of Economics and Finance*, published online, November 2020. www.sciencedirect.com/science/article/abs/pii/S1062976920301496

McCauley, R. (2018) The 2008 crisis: transatlantic or transpacific?, *BIS Quarterly Review*, December.

Medvedev, D. (2009) *For a more diversified international financial system*, Yekaterinburg, 15 August.

Merton, R.C. and Brodie, Z. (1995) A conceptual framework for analyzing the financial environment. In *The Global Financial System: A Functional Perspective*, edited by D. Crane. Boston: Harvard Business School, pp 3–12.

Minsky, H. (1977) A theory of systemic fragility. In *Financial Crises: Institutions and Markets in a Fragile Environment*, edited by E. Altman and A.W. Sametx. New York: Wiley, pp 138–152.

Minsky, H. (1982) *Can 'It' Happen Again?*, New York: M.E. Sharpe.

Minsky, H. (1986) *Stabilizing an Unstable Economy*, New Haven: Yale University Press.

Munchau, W. (2023) Why China and her allies are well placed to topple the dollar, *New Statesman*, 3 May.

OECD (Organisation for Economic Co-operation and Development) (2019a) *Pension Markets in Focus*, Paris: OECD Publishing.

OECD (2019b) *Social Expenditure Update*.

OECD (2020a) The world economy on a tightrope, *OECD Economic Outlook*, June.

OECD (2020b) *Sovereign Borrowing Outlook*, July.

OECD (2021) *Sovereign Borrowing Outlook*, July.

OECD (2022) *Sovereign Borrowing Outlook*, July.

Osborne, G. (2010) *A New Economic Framework*. Mais Lecture, Bayes Business School, City University of London, 24 February.

Papa, M. and Liu, Z.Z. (2022) *Can BRICS De-dollarize the Global Financial System?*, Cambridge: Cambridge University Press and Assessment.

Piketty, T. (2014) *Capital in the 21st Century*, Cambridge, MA: Harvard University Press.

Pöhl, K.O. (1995) International monetary policy: a personal view. In *Russian Reform/International Money*, edited by E.T. Gaidar and K.O. Pöhl. Cambridge, MA and London: MIT Press, pp 55–140.

Prasad, E. (2014) *The Dollar Trap: How the U.S. Dollar Tightened Its Grip on Global Finance*, Princeton: Princeton University Press.

Prasad, E. (2018) America beware: dollar supremacy is not forever, *Financial Times*, 20 May.

Pozsar, Z. (2023) Great power conflict puts the dollar's exorbitant privilege under threat, *Financial Times*, 20 January.

Rajan, R.G. (2010) *Fault Lines*, Princeton: Princeton University Press.

Reinhart, C. and Rogoff, K. (2010) Growth in a time of debt, NBER Working Paper 15639.

Rinaldi, R. and Santini, C. (1998) Italy: two foreign exchange crises. In *Financial Crisis Management in Regional Blocs*, edited by S.S. Rehman. New York: Springer, pp 55–94.

Roubini, N. (2023) A bipolar currency regime will replace the dollar's exorbitant privilege, *Financial Times*, 5 February.

Sawyer, M. (2022) *Financialization*, Newcastle upon Tyne: Agenda Publishing.

SIFMA (Securities Industry and Financial Markets Association) (2022) *US Fact Book*.

SIFMA (2023) *Capital Markets Fact Book*.

SIPRI (Stockholm International Peace Research Institute) (2023) *SIPRI Yearbook: Armaments, Disarmament and International Security*, Stockholm: SIPRI.

Stiglitz, J.E. (2016) *The Euro: How a Common Currency Threatens the Future of Europe*, New York: W.W. Norton.

Stone, I. (1999) *The Global Export of Capital From Great Britain, 1865–1914*, Basingstoke and London: Macmillan Press.

Tanzi, V. (1999) The demise of the nation state? In *Globalisation and Labour*, edited by H. Siebert. Tubingen: Kiel Institute of World Economics, pp 293–312.

Tanzi, V. and Schuknecht, L. (2000) *Public Spending in the 20th Century*, Cambridge: Cambridge University Press.

Tett, G. (2023) Prepare for a multipolar currency world, *Financial Times*, 30 March.

Thompson, H. (2022) *Disorder: Hard Times in the 21st Century*, Oxford: Oxford University Press.

van Apeldoorn, B. and de Graaf, N. (2022) The state in global capitalism before and after the Covid-19 crisis, *Contemporary Politics*, 28(3): 306–327.

Van der Zwan, N. (2014) Making sense of financialization, *Socio-Economic Review*, 12: 99–129.

Vercelli, A. (2013) Financialization in a long run perspective, *International Journal of Political Economy*, 42: 19–46.

Wheatley, A. (2013) The pretenders to the dollar's crown. In *The Power of Currencies and Currencies of Power*, edited by A. Wheatley. New York: Routledge and the International Institute for Strategic Studies, pp 45–73.

Whitley, R. (1999) *Divergent Capitalisms: The Social Structuring and Change of Business Systems*, Oxford: Oxford University Press.

Wolf, M. (2004) America on the comfortable path to ruin, *Financial Times*, 17 August.

Index

F

Printed and bound by CPI Group (UK) Ltd, Croydon, CR0 4YY

15/09/2026

14962388-0001